DO NOT REMOVE
CARDS FROM POCKET

ALLEN COUNTY PUBLIC LIBRARY

FORT WAYNE, INDIANA 46802

You may return this book to any agency, branch,
or bookmobile of the Allen County Public Library.

What's Wrong, Who's Right in Central America?

What's Wrong, Who's Right in **Central America?**

A Citizen's Guide

Richard A. Nuccio
Roosevelt Center for American Policy Studies
with research by Kelly A. McBride

Facts On File Publications
New York, New York • Oxford, England

Library of Congress Cataloging-in-Publication Data

Nuccio, Richard.
   What's wrong, who's right in Central America?

   Bibliography: p.
   Includes index.
   1. Central America—Politics and government—
1979- . I. Title.
F1439.5.N83 1986   972.8'053   85-31093
ISBN 0-8160-1374-8

Printed in the United States of America

10   9   8   7   6   5   4   3   2

To my son, Erin, who makes it all worthwhile

*To my parents, who believed in the higher education
they never had the opportunity to pursue, and to my grandmother,
who made it possible for me*

Contents

Preface

Central America is not just for specialists. It should be of concern to everyone who cares about the issues of peace and war. In Central America organized violence by forces of the right and left has cost the lives of over 100,000 people during the last seven years. President Reagan has defined what happens in the region as of vital interest to the United States. Yet opinion polls continue to confirm that nearly three-fourths of those questioned do not know which side the United States supports—the government or its armed opposition—in the key countries of El Salvador and Nicaragua.

What's Wrong, Who's Right in Central America? was not written to support or to oppose official policy in Central America. It is designed to provide average citizens with basic information and analysis that will allow them to make their own judgments about what U.S. policy in the region should be. The Roosevelt Center, as a nonpartisan, nonadvocacy institution, has no particular axe to grind in the making of U.S. Central American policy. But we do believe that what happens in that part of the world will affect the future of U.S. relations with all of Latin America and help to determine how the United States will deal with social change in Third World countries—a challenge that will confront U.S. foreign policy for decades to come.

The organization of the book merits a brief comment. This introduction to Central America begins with two vignettes designed to paint a verbal picture of two very different kinds of realities in El Salvador and Nicaragua. Chapter 1 is the briefest of summaries of the history of the entire Central American region up to the 1970s. Chapter 2 focuses on the five individual countries of Nicaragua, El Salvador, Honduras, Costa Rica, and Guatemala in "snapshots" that update political developments to late 1985. Chapter 3 is a guide to the policy debate as it occurs in Washington for each of the five countries told from the perspectives of a "national security analyst" and a "human rights activist." Chapter 4 gives some examples of how citizens have organized themselves to support or oppose current policy toward Central America.

This book owes a debt to a great many people, only some of whom can be acknowledged. Howard Wiarda, who taught my first class on Latin American politics, and many thereafter, is probably quoted verbatim at times in Chapter 1 without my knowing it! Abraham Lowenthal was an early guide to holding conflicting ideas in one's head simultaneously even before I had the chance to see him do it firsthand during his stewardship of the Latin American Program at the Wilson Center. Amando de Miguel, the Spanish sociologist, showed me that "popularizing" ideas did not necessarily demean them. All of these mentors thought I had a book in me; it was a long time getting out.

Numerous friends and colleagues read early drafts of the manuscript. William Leo Grande and Virginia Polk were particularly generous with their time and were constructively critical. Carlos Egan made detailed comments and posed some hard questions as only a good friend can. Peter Hakim gave attention to substance and style. Cynthia Aronson lent her considerable expertise on El Salvador. Alexander Wilde helped defeat an unwise tentative title. As should be evident to anyone who knows these individuals, their often conflicting advice could not always be incorporated. But they helped to keep me on track and to avoid most, but not all, errors.

My colleagues at the Roosevelt Center provided just the right combination of carrot and stick to produce the book only slightly behind schedule. Christopher Makins, director of international security studies, made detailed comments and offered broad encouragement. If his proper British demeanor permitted it, I would give him a warm, Latin *abrazo*.

Kelly McBride, director of research for the project, kept the pile of Central America material flowing across my desk and into files where it could be retrieved. She added her own firsthand experience in El Salvador and Nicaragua to Chapters 2 and 4. She worked closely with me on the design and conception of the book and her contributions are greatly appreciated.

Chris Namerdy put much of the original manuscript onto the word processor and helped to coordinate its production. Roger Kittleson was an invaluable intern during the last hectic phases of the book.

Thanks are especially due to the many Central Americans who offered their insights and experiences to a curious gringo, as well as to Janet Shenk, my first guide to the intrigues of Central America.

Impressions gathered during that first visit contributed to the vignettes with which the book begins.

Richard A. Nuccio
December, 1985

Prologue

EL SALVADOR: NO NEUTRAL GROUND

The refugee camp outside San Martín del Campo holds 5,000 human souls in barely human conditions. Houses are thatched huts with packed earthen floors supported by wooden poles. Foul water comes from a single pipe at the end of a muddy pathway; bathrooms are ditches cut in the dirt at the edge of the camp.

María is a leader of sorts in the camp. She has lived in one of these huts for nearly three years, since she fled the war in the eastern province of her country. She has special responsibilities as *botiquín*, the dispenser of basic medicines to combat diarrhea and the tubercular coughs that afflict many, especially the old. Being a *botiquín* is dangerous for María: she has medicine, a valuable commodity, and the local soldiers will always wonder if she passes it on to the subversives. She gets her supplies from the local religious lay workers; the army thinks they are subversives too.

As María talks, an eleven-month-old with a dirty face and only a tee-shirt for clothing toddles back and forth across the hut, crawling into his mother's lap to suck at her breast from time to time. He is the youngest of seven; the oldest is dead.

"He was a good boy. I still miss him so. He worked hard and tried to be someone. But they wouldn't leave him alone. He made friends with the police, and they taught him a skill. He learned to type, and each day he worked at the police station filling in reports on the machine. He typed so well and never made a mistake.

"But the guerrillas called him a collaborator, and one night they came and took him away. I don't know what they did to him there. He was not against the guerrillas, he was not for the police. We only want to live and work. We don't want to choose to fight and die.

"They kept him for two weeks. I didn't know what had happened to him. But they let him go or he escaped. People saw him coming down from the mountains. If he had come back, I would have made him leave here. Perhaps to go to the capital; maybe to try to make it to the United States. He was a good boy. He knew how to work hard.

"But he never made it back to us. A patrol of customs police saw him coming from the guerrilla area. They thought he was a subversive. They didn't believe that he was just my son, just a peasant boy, the joy of his mother. They tied his thumbs behind his back, and they shot him.

"Some say that death is peaceful. I do not believe that it is so. My son's face had the look of terror on it. I hope that God will give him the peace he did not have here. I hope that God will give us all peace."

NICARAGUA: CAPTURING THE PRIVATE SECTOR

The lunch of beans, rice, roasted pork, and salad was even more delicious taken in the sun-drenched courtyard of the coffeegrower's home. But we were not satisfied. The loyal coffeegrowers of Matagalpa had told us more of what we had been hearing from official spokespersons about the wonders of *Sandinismo*. We had come to this village birthplace of the Sandinista movement to meet with that elusive private sector, threatened but still surviving in "pluralist" Nicaragua. These men, owners of coffee plantations not nationalized by the government, represented the small-scale businesses that were being tolerated in Nicaragua's mixed economy of capitalism and socialism.

Some of the men looked and acted the part: uncomfortable in front of a group of foreigners, they seemed like hard-working farmer-entrepreneurs from any part of the world. Those who did the most talking, however, were clearly businessmen turned loyal politicians. Their praise of the revolution, with the familiar admission of "errors," seemed rehearsed. The members of our delegation shifted uneasily in their seats.

In the small groups that formed over lunch, we pressed some of the growers: Is everyone so enthusiastic about the Sandinistas? Could we meet growers who were not happy with the changes?

"Yes, perhaps that could be arranged," said one of the growers who had been especially quiet during the litany of praise. The largest grower in Matagalpa lived in town; he might be willing to see us.

The house of the richest grower was impressive even by North American standards. Constructed in Spanish style, its interior of tile and mosaic was cool and inviting. We seated ourselves next to a modern kitchen inside a room furnished with outdoor furniture. An expensive stereo played classical music in the background.

"I am the president of the coffeegrowers of this region and I have been a grower all my life. I have stayed in Nicaragua because this is my home. I did not allow Somoza to drive me from my home; I will not allow the Sandinistas to do it either.

"I am committed to the future. You saw the big Bank of America building on your way into town. I will borrow $100,000 from the Bank of America this year to plant new trees. These will not produce for a number of years. But if the Sandinistas let me, I will be here to pay off the loan.

"How is business? Not good. The government controls everything; my profits are worse than under Somoza. They tell me to whom I must sell and at what prices. Because of their fight with the United States, I can't get many of the imports I need. Sometimes I think that the government doesn't care about producing coffee. All they care about is Sandino.

"Yes, I criticize the government here in my home with Americans who need to know about our country. But it is dangerous. A friend's land was confiscated recently because he opposed the government. When you complain, they say you are a *contra* and take your land.

"But I still hope things will change. I don't like dictatorships of the right or the left. I want a free market, free schools, and a free church. When we were in Guatemala we had good church schools. Here they are trying to fill them up with Sandinista propaganda. And the church. There should be only one church for rich and poor. I don't believe in this people's church. Just one church.

"The poor are worse off now than they were under Somoza. Ask Pablito [the small grower who led us to the large grower's house and who now sits deferentially at his side]. He is a good worker; he rents land from me. Tell them how the peasants eat worse now than before."

"Well, Don Rodrigo, I'm not sure. You know, before there was much injustice and now the workers have at least the..."

"Nonsense, Pablito. The peasants were better off before the Sandinistas. On my farms we always had schools for the workers, took care of them, helped them when they had problems. Now they are worse off, don't you agree, Pablito?"

"Perhaps, Don Rodrigo, but also..."

"Absolutely. And if you say the truth they send the *turbas* [mobs] to attack you. You see that hole in the window? That is where the *turbas* attacked my house. This is *Sandinismo*."

As we leave the house, the young Nicaraguan lay worker for a Protestant church who has been accompanying us is downcast and sullen. The son of uneducated parents, he was identified at an early age as a natural leader and now at eighteen coordinates Protestant welfare projects throughout the northern provinces where he was born. Earlier in understated simplicity he had told us of the desperate conditions under which the poor with whom he works must live and how *Sandinismo* has meant improvement in the lives of many for the first time. Now his voice has an edge that we have not heard before.

"It was men like him who ruled my mother and father until they died. I grew up on a coffee plantation. We had no school; we had no doctor. People like him disgust me; they think they know everything. I wonder when he ever leaves this mansion to see how we peasants live on his wonderful farms?"

Months later, back in that other world called Washington, the note arrived. Our guide in Nicaragua thought we would want to know that the grower in whose house we shared lunch had been killed in the civil war. His severed head was left in the central plaza as a warning to others who collaborate with the Sandinistas. Perhaps we would want to protest the atrocity to the United States government, which supports the opposition *contras*. Perhaps.

What's Wrong, Who's Right
in **Central America?**

Central America
from Columbus to Castro

The "Black Legend" is about the original "evil empire." It is that set of truths, half-truths, and non-truths that the British created to justify their attacks on the Spanish empire many centuries ago. According to the "Black Legend," the Spanish were vile men possessed of evil notions of government who needed to be vanquished by the superior and enlightened British. All manner of outrages perpetrated by the British against the Spanish were legitimated by this "Black Legend."

The Spanish, for their part, came to view the Anglo-Saxons as the natural enemy of everything for which Spanish civilization stood. The fact that one country, Spain, saw itself as the defender of the true faith and the other, England, as a defender of Protestantism made their enmity all the more bitter. From that time to the present day, the Spanish have viewed with suspicion and hostility any criticism by Anglo-Saxons, including the North American variety, of their values and institutions. They see such criticism as a continuation of that "Black Legend" that had charged the Spanish with roasting heretics for breakfast.

To understand what is happening today in Central America, one must go back to the origins of these societies and to the values, attitudes, and institutions that Spain bequeathed to the nations of the New World. For North Americans it is helpful to contrast the founding of our own society in the seventeenth century with the founding of Latin America a century earlier. But it is important to do so without perpetuating the myths of the "Black Legend" that the "superiority"of the Anglo-Saxon race explains the different histories of Central America and the United States since each gained its independence.

"Central America is America; it's at our doorstep."
—President Ronald Reagan, May 1984

Central Americans themselves have a certain ambivalence about their Spanish ancestors. Their societies would not exist in their current form were it not for the Spanish. Yet those societies were created as a result of the conquest of native peoples who in some parts of Central America had highly developed civilizations of their own. The traces of those native peoples can be seen in the faces of most of the inhabitants of Central America and heard in the myriad native languages that still prevail in many of the rural areas. The legacy of the destruction of these native civilizations is also evident in the land tenure system and the pattern of violence that make contemporary politics in Central America so vicious. The essence of Central America lies in its being a mixture of the Old World and the New. But at times many Central Americans wonder if they have adopted not the best but the worst of both.

THE FOUNDING OF THE AMERICAS, NORTH AND SOUTH

The beginnings of what became the United States and the nations of Central America were very different. These two parts of the Americas were colonized more than a century apart and presented distinct environments to the colonizer. There were also differences in the characters of the men who came to the New World and in the values they brought with them.

Seventeenth-century England was a country on the verge of the social, political, and economic revolution—the Industrial Revolution—that created the modern world as we know it. English settlers in North America came from a modernizing England that generally treated literacy, toleration, individual rights, economic liberty, saving, and investment as inseparable elements of a process of change and growth. Sixteenth-century Spain was, on the other hand, a country struggling to emerge from the Dark Ages. Only recently reunited as a nation, Spain would spend the sixteenth and seventeenth centuries defending the traditional values of a monolithic Catholic Church, an authoritarian government, and an aristocratic order. While many English settlers in the New World came in search of religious freedom, Spanish conquerors imposed a purified Catholicism on the indigenous population.

The early settlers in North and South America encountered very different environments. The first English company charters provided for the discovery of precious-metal mines, but no mines were found. While Spanish conquerors to the south searched for El Dorado, the mythical city of gold, the English colonists established the small family farms that were suited to the ecology of the North American east coast. If the English had discovered mineral riches, they would have had no indigenous source of labor to exploit them. Europeans in North America did not have to confront or incorporate substantial Indian cultures as was the case in much of Central America. Indian culture was then, as it is today, irrelevant for the white society. The nomadic American Indian inhabitants were pushed aside, killed, or isolated as survivors on unproductive lands. The Spaniards, on the other hand, faced huge native populations that numbered in the tens of millions and lived a sedentary and, in some cases, highly civilized life. The temptation of the Spaniards to eliminate the native elite while leaving intact an authoritarian structure of exploitation of the population mass proved too great to resist.

These accidents of history had profound implications for the future of the two colonial areas. The story of Pocahontas, the Indian princess who converted to Christianity and married an Englishman, is part of North American mythology. But such an event was relatively rare. Because of the small numbers and nomadic existence of the North American Indians, white and Indian societies remained relatively isolated and racially distinct. In Mexico and Central America, the Spanish brought few women with them and intermarriage with the native population became commonplace. Demographic disaster from disease and brutal exploitation reduced the Indians' numbers dramatically in the first few decades after the conquest and set the stage for the creation of the distinctive *mestizo* (mixed) society that still characterizes parts of Central America today. In this *mestizo* society, a tiny Spanish elite ruled over a dwindling Indian peasantry and a growing mixed lower and middle class. *Pureza de sangre* (purity of blood) became the trait that separated rich from poor, powerful from powerless. These racial divisions that became class and caste divisions would create barriers, which did not have to be faced in North America, to social mobility, income distribution, and to the very idea of national identity.

Nowhere in the New World except in North America did there exist a huge, accessible, underpopulated, virgin land of extraordinary resources that enjoyed a climate comparable to that of Europe. It was not surprising then that the North American colonists established different land-tenure patterns from those in Central America.

The special social structure and land-tenure pattern that characterized Central America was encouraged by the existence of a servile population suitable for slave labor, of mines that needed to be worked, and of a climate conducive to a plantation-type economy. Unlike North America where family farms predominated, Central America was characterized by large-scale enterprises that placed the privileged white Spaniards in charge of the exploited native masses in mines, on *haciendas*, and, eventually, on export-oriented plantations.

The pattern of these early economies had profound implications for the future political structures of the Central American countries. Mining and large-scale agriculture produced a two-class society where a few used political power to control and exploit the many. The middle class, so important in moderating tension between rich and poor in democratic countries, remained small and politically unimportant until well into the twentieth century in most of Central America. The monopoly of wealth held by the upper class distorted political development, as the Central American elite fought tooth and nail to resist change that would force them to share their power with those lower on the social scale.

In that part of North America most similiar in climate to Latin America, the antebellum South, plantation economies based on the exploitation of imported slave labor did develop along with an aristocratic lifestyle and social differentiation of a racial kind. The tension between an industrial, relatively egalitarian North and an agricultural, slave-holding South eventually produced a cataclysmic civil war in the United States. We can gain some sense of the problems facing Central America today by speculating on what the United States would look like if the South rather than the North had won the war; if slavery, rather than being abolished, had been extended; and if the Southern aristocracy had maintained its political domination for ninety more years. Despite the crushing defeat of the South's social system in the Civil War, the heritage of slavery, racial discrimination, and plantation agriculture would continue to retard the development of the South for nearly a century. Only after the Second World War would the New South of industry and progress begin to emerge. Most of Latin America has never fought this kind of civil war to defeat a political and economic system based on the exploitation of peasant labor.

Central America entered the era of political independence with its colonial heritage bearing down upon it. For a variety of internal and external reasons, societies had been created that were highly unequal and authoritarian, largely agricultural, and dependent on the outside world for many of the products necessary to their existence. It was not a propitious way to begin life as independent nations, and the manner in which that independence came to Central America set even more roadblocks on the path to a prosperous and democratic future.

INDEPENDENCE: RUNNING AWAY FROM CHANGE

Independence came to Mexico and Central America not as a struggle to preserve freedom from European tyranny, but as a way for con-servative elites in the colonies to preserve their privileges from democratic reforms occurring in mother Spain. In Spain, in 1812, a Liberal constitution had been written that provided for a limited monarchy, promised freedom of speech and assembly, and abolished the Inquisition. Initially suppressed by the Spanish King Ferdinand VII, the constitution was restored in 1820 and threatened to under-mine the position of the colonial elite.

By the time of independence, most Central American countries were divided into four distinct social groups. The *peninsulares*, or peninsulars, were native-born Spaniards whose purity of blood and connections to the crown gave them positions of privilege in the colonies in business, trade, and politics. The *criollos*, or creoles, were pure-blooded Spaniards who had been born in America and occupied the next rung of society. Ambitious and conscious of their social status, they resented the *peninsulares* and wished to replace them as the dominant group. *Ladinos*, or people of mixed blood, ranged in social status from a relatively well-off middle class to an impoverished underclass in the cities and rural areas. Aggressive and socially mobile, they formed the shock troops in the civil wars that were to follow independence. The Indians occupied the bottom rung of the social ladder and were abused and exploited by all those above them. Largely excluded from national economic and political life, they turned inward and focused on the family, the village, and the region.

Independence movements that had real mass support and promised to improve the lot of the Indians and *ladinos*, such as that led by Father Hidalgo in Mexico in 1810, were promptly and brutally put down by a coalition of *peninsulares* and *criollos*. Only when events in Spain raised the specter of change from above did the Mexican creole elite decide to back a movement for independence. In the region that became Central America, independence was even more half-hearted. A Mexican general, Iturbide, declared himself emperor of Mexico and threatened to "liberate" Central America by force in 1821. Faced with attack from without or a self-proclaimed independence, the future United Provinces of Central America declared independence. With independence came the kind of bitter partisan debate that would consume Central America for the next thirty years. Different factions of the elite argued the merits of being an independent republic versus annexing themselves to Mexico. Once again events in Mexico forced decisions on the Central Americans. Iturbide's abdication in 1823 led to the proclamation of absolute Central American independence on July 1 of the same year. Only Chiapas elected to remain with Mexico to become the southernmost state of the Mexican federation.

The United Provinces of Central America, what we now know as Guatemala, Honduras, Nicaragua, El Salvador, and Costa Rica, began independent life with a number of strikes against them. Superficial social changes such as the end of the Inquisition, the elimination of legal discrimination on the basis of race, and the abolition of titles of nobility did occur. But independence left the existing economic and social structures intact. This was not surprising, for the creole elite that headed the movement had no intention of transforming the existing order. They sought to replace the *peninsulares* in the seats of power and to break the monopoly of trade held by Spain, not to change the labor and land systems. As producers of raw materials and foodstuffs for sale in the markets of Europe and North America, the plantation owners' interests required the maintenance of the system of great estates worked by a semiservile native population. No agrarian reform accompanied independence. The plantations abandoned by or confiscated from the loyalist Spaniards were often appropriated by the new creole aristocracy.

Central Americans had avoided a war with Mexico or with Spain in becoming independent. They could not avoid forever the pressures for social change that had been building in the final years of the colonial era. In the decades after independence, Central Americans should have engaged in the difficult process of nation building. Instead, they found themselves in a series of bitter civil wars that left the new governments impoverished and established a pattern of instability that has continued to the present.

CONSERVATIVES VS. LIBERALS: TWO IDEALS IN SEARCH OF REALITY

There is no better introduction to the confusing civil wars of the early years of independence in Latin America than this dialogue from *One Hundred Years of Solitude*, the epic novel of the Colombian novelist Gabriel García Márquez:

On one occasion on the eve of the elections, Don Apolinar Moscote returned from one of his frequent trips worried about the political situation in the country. The Liberals were determined to go to war. Since Aureliano at that time had very confused notions about the difference between Conservatives and Liberals, his father-in-law gave him some schematic lessons. The Liberals, he said, were Freemasons, bad people, wanting to hang priests, to institute civil marriage and divorce, to recognize the rights of illegitimate children as equal to those of legitimate ones, and to cut the country up into a federal system that would take power away from the supreme authority. The Conservatives, on the other hand, who had received their power directly from God, proposed the establishment of public order and family morality. They were the defenders of the faith of Christ, of the principle of authority, and were not prepared to permit the country to be broken down into autonomous entities. Because of his humanitarian feelings, Aureliano sympathized with the Liberal attitude with respect to the rights of natural children, but in any case, he could not understand how people arrived at the extreme of waging war over things that could not be touched with the hand.

* * *

The elections took place without incident. At eight o'clock on Sunday morning, a wooden ballot box was set up in the square, which was watched over by the six soldiers. The voting was absolutely free, as Aureliano himself was able to attest since he spent almost the entire day with his father-in-law seeing that no one voted more than once. At four in the afternoon a roll of drums in the square announced the closing of the polls and Don Apolinar Moscote sealed the ballot box with a label crossed by his signature. That night, while he played dominoes with Aureliano, he ordered the sergeant to break the seal in order to count the votes. There were almost as many red ballots as blue, but the sergeant left only ten red ones and made up the difference with blue ones. Then they sealed the box again with a new label and the first thing on the following day it was taken to the capital of the province. "The Liberals will go to war," Aureliano said. Don Apolinar concentrated on his domino pieces. "If you're saying that because of the switch in ballots, they won't," he said. "We left a few red ones in so there won't be any complaints." Aureliano understood the disadvantages of being in the opposition. "If I were a Liberal," he said, "I'd go to war because of those ballots." His father-in-law looked at him over his glasses.

"Come now, Aurelito," he said, "if you were a Liberal, even though you're my son-in-law, you wouldn't have seen the switching of the ballots."

Colonel Aureliano Buendía, having learned these lessons about the realities of power, goes on to fight and lose thirty-two wars between the Liberals and Conservatives. Leaders change sides, betray their principles, and rejoin once-spurned colleagues in García Márquez's masterpiece until it seems that political ideology serves as no more than a pretext for ritualistic warfare, a kind of Latin American version of the Hatfields and McCoys. Yet in almost all Latin American countries, and especially in Central America, the decades after independence were a time of partisan battles between Liberals and Conservatives.

In a sense, the way in which Central America became independent produced the period of civil wars. At its end, the Spanish imperial system was clearly not working well for either the colonizers or the colonized. Yet, instead of replacing it, independence movements in Central America attempted to preserve the essence of the old system while channeling benefits that used to go to the Spaniards to the newly dominant creole elite. Divisions within that elite and between the elite and the other classes were not reconciled as they might have been in a national struggle for independence. Rather, they were postponed, to be fought out when Central Americans had to decide what kind of independence they were to have. Should the new states preserve the traditional way of life, modifying and adapting the colonial heritage to changing circumstances, as Conservatives argued? Or should Central America cast off the burden of the Iberian heritage and embrace republican innovations from France, England, and the United States? Basic and provocative issues were at stake. What should be the position of the Catholic Church in independent Central America? Should there be a strong central government as Conservatives wanted or a federation with weak central powers? Free trade, the Liberals argued, would lead to great advances for the Central American economies. Conservatives countered, correctly as it turned out, that unrestricted trade would cripple local industry and merchants who had long operated behind protective trade barriers.

Liberals, in particular, were attracted to the vision of Central America described by Simón Bolívar, the liberator of South America, as early as 1815:

The States of the Isthmus from Panama to Guatemala will perhaps form a confederation. This magnificent location between the two great oceans could in time become the emporium of the world. Its canals will shorten the distances throughout the world, strengthen commercial ties with Europe, America, and Asia, and bring that happy region tribute from the four quarters of the globe. Perhaps some day the capital of the world may be located there, just as Constantine claimed Byzantium as the capital of the ancient world.

The apparent success of England's former colonies in North America influenced political debates in Central America. Liberals argued that a confederation of the Central American states based on the North American model and constitution would guarantee Bolívar's vision of a glorious future for the region. Conservatives wanted a unitary system as had existed in colonial times. Liberals, although strongly Catholic in their personal beliefs, wanted to abolish church privileges (called *fueros*) and confiscate religious wealth. Conservatives upheld the religious and educational monopoly of the Roman Catholic Church and supported the *fueros* of the church and the military. Each side launched into civil war to press its case when excluded from power and ruthlessly suppressed its opponents when in power. Although fighting bitterly for the most high-minded political principles, each side used quite similar authoritarian methods to maintain themselves in power. The conditions of war put a premium on military prowess rather than on statesmanship and ushered in the strongman on horseback, or *caudillo*, who through charisma, manipulation of the masses, or both, succeeded for a time in enforcing order.

Divisions along ideological lines were reinforced by regional differences as the United Provinces began to fly apart. Rule by one element of the Liberal or Conservative faction in the capital of the federation would be opposed by their counterparts in some outlying state. By the mid-1840s, the combination of war and economic decline had put an end to Bolívar's dream of a united federation of Central American states. Unity would be an aspiration of future Central American leaders down to the present, but an unrealizable one.

It is hard to imagine a worse beginning for a newly independent region than that experienced by Central America in the thirty years after independence. Liberals and Conservatives held mutually exclusive visions of how Central American society should be organized. Although the Liberals carried the banner of change and progress, their ideals rarely coincided with Central American realities. Their free-trade policies destroyed native industry. The breakup of Catholic Church-held lands, designed, Liberals argued, to improve the efficiency of agriculture and end the dominance of rural areas by the few, resulted in an even tighter concentration of land (in the Liberal elite's hands, of course) and the elimination of many traditional holdings of Indian groups. In their desperation to counter Conservative policies and influence, the Liberals adopted highly authoritarian measures that violated many of their republican principles.

Neither Liberals nor Conservatives ever developed a vision of society that included all groups and classes. Their struggles ultimately appeared as disputes among different sectors of a privileged elite for the right to continue to benefit from the exploitation of the many. Although Liberals and Conservatives often dominated politics in some of the Central American countries for long periods, neither side achieved complete success for its ideas or programs. Perhaps it would have been better for Central America in the long run to have seen the triumph of any one plan for the future, either Liberal or Conservative. Instead, the two sides wore each other down to a state of mutual exhaustion (and the financial bankruptcy of many governments). In the absence of a final victory, that peculiar amalgam that strikes all visitors to Latin America was created. In what has been called Latin America's "living museum," ideas from all ages and ideologies coexist, none dominant, none replacing the other, none providing a coherent model to be followed. This is the special fascination of Latin America, but also its greatest weakness. The decades after independence in Central America witnessed much revolt but no revolution, no dramatic shift from old ideas and structures to new. Without a vision of the future, Central America soon reverted to its past of internal weakness and dependence on the new outside powers who were to replace Spain: first England and then the United States.

FROM COLONY TO INDEPENDENCE TO NEOCOLONY

Another passage from *One Hundred Years of Solitude* describes much of Latin America's perception of the United States:

> The gringos, who later on brought their languid wives in muslin dresses and large veiled hats, built a separate town across the railroad tracks with streets lined with palm trees, houses with screened windows, small white tables on the terraces, and fans mounted on the ceilings, and extensive blue lawns with peacocks and quails. The section was surrounded by a metal fence topped with a band of electrified chicken wire which during

the cool summer mornings would be black with roasted swallows. No one knew yet what they were after, or whether they were actually nothing but philanthropists, and they had already caused a colossal disturbance, much more than that of the old gypsies, but less transitory and understandable. Endowed with means that had been reserved for Divine Providence in former times, they changed the pattern of the rains, accelerated the cycle of harvest, and moved the river from where it had always been and put it with its white stones and icy currents on the other side of the town, behind the cemetery....

"Look at the mess we've got ourselves into," Colonel Aureliano Buendía said at that time, "just because we invited a gringo[2] to eat some bananas."

There are probably as many stories about the origin of the word *gringo* to refer to English-speaking foreigners in Latin America as there are Latin Americans. Some say it came from the soldiers' marching songs during an invasion of Mexico when they sang "Green grow the lilacs," as they paraded in the capital. Others contend that the soldiers' green uniforms inspired the term. But all versions of its origin agree that it was coined to express popular hatred for the strange and arrogant northerners whom the Latin Americans and particularly the Central Americans found increasingly in their midst in the last half of the nineteenth century.

Most North Americans,[3] who are innocent of the deeds that promoted this hostility and may be ignorant of the history of their country's relations with Central America, understandably respond defensively to popular attitudes toward the "Colossus of the North," as the United States is unaffectionately known. They would find the unflattering portrait of the *gringos* painted by García Márquez as unfair and overdrawn and be amused that the Latins viewed Yankee ingenuity as "means that had been reserved for Divine Providence in former times." These attitudes are, however, an essential part of Central America's history and are basic to understanding United States-Central American relations today.

It is perhaps easier to understand the sensitive nature of United States-Central American relations if one remembers that the Central Americans thought, naively as it turned out, that their independence would produce the kinds of advances that they had witnessed after the independence of North America. It was doubly hard to accept their own failures when they saw a country they had admired and, in some cases, tried to imitate, advancing beyond them and, ultimately, becoming a new imperial power.

This region of the world has always been an object of special attention for the United States. As a weak naval power and a relatively poor country, the United States did not provide much assistance to the independence movements in Latin America. From 1819 to 1821, a critical juncture for the independence movement, the United States was involved in delicate negotiations with Spain for the purchase of Florida and steered clear of any challenge to Spanish prerogatives in the region. But in one of its first major foreign policy initiatives, the United States placed itself on the side of independence, once achieved, in Latin America. On December 2, 1823, President James Monroe declared that, as a matter of principle, "the American continents, by the free and independent condition they have assumed and maintain, are henceforth not to be considered subjects for future colonization by any European powers....We should consider any attempt on their [the European powers'] part to extend their system to any portion of this hemisphere as dangerous to our peace and safety." For its part, the United States pledged not to interfere with existing colonies nor to "meddle" in European affairs.

This Monroe Doctrine, as it was called, was largely ineffective for most of the nineteenth century, as the United States had neither the resources nor the determination to carry it out. But Great Britain, which did have a powerful fleet and a virtual monopoly of trade in the area, had an interest in blocking other European competitors. Although no formal colonies were reestablished, British and French gunboats regularly bombarded or blockaded Latin American ports to force payment of debts or reparations, without any response on the part of the United States.

Despite the high-minded statements about preserving Latin American independence, one can fairly describe the Monroe Doctrine as a way to close off Latin America to "outside" powers, while leaving the area open to intervention by the United States. This intervention was not only through trade, but included the landing of troops in the Falkland/Malvinas Islands, Argentina, and Peru during the 1830s; in Argentina, Nicaragua, Uruguay, Panama, Paraguay, and Mexico during the 1850s; and in Panama, Uruguay, Mexico, and Colombia during the 1860s. Many Latin Americans began to worry about the intentions of the United States after the maneuvers to separate Texas from Mexico and eventually annex it and after the "trumped-up war," as the young Abraham Lincoln called it, that appropriated the territories of Arizona, New Mexico, and California from Mexico in 1846-1847. Barely a half-century old, the United States had successfully waged a war of territorial acquisition against Mexico, its closest Latin neighbor. It was following, editorial writers of the day argued, its Manifest Destiny.[4]

In Central America, the mid-1800s were the age of the filibuster, or independent soldier of fortune. None would be more picturesque than William Walker, the "grey-eyed man of destiny." A historical marker in Memphis, Tennessee, tells the essential facts of his life: "Born May 8,

1824. In early life he was a doctor, lawyer, and journalist. He invaded Mexico in 1853 with 46 men and proclaimed himself President, Republic of Lower California. Led force into Nicaragua in 1855; was elected its President in 1856. In attempt to wage war on Honduras was captured and executed September 12, 1860."

Central American politics had become so out of control that adventurers like Walker with a few dozen men could tip the balance between Conservatives and Liberals and were often invited to do so by one side or the other. The interventionist designs of the United States and other powers complicated the politics of Central America in tragic ways, but they only took advantage of the failure of Central America's leaders to develop strong and effective political and economic systems that would discourage outside meddling.

The Liberals came to dominate most Central American countries in the last third of the nineteenth century. Their earlier concern for political freedom had now been supplanted by a preoccupation with material progress. New constitutions paid lip service to the republican principles of earlier Liberals, but in fact provided for centralized, executive-dominated governments with the military as the real arbiter of public affairs. In the ultimate irony, the triumph of Liberalism would be known as the Age of the Dictatorships.

In the continuing Central American fascination with importing ideas as well as luxury goods from Europe, the Liberals promoted the ideal of positivism, or the belief that science should rule the conduct of society. The idea of applying Darwin's theory of evolution to the social order prompted a concern with the "survival of the fittest" in Central America. The "fit" were, not unexpectedly, the more white and European elements in society. These elements were to be encouraged through domestic economic policies that would reward the aggressive and ambitious. Immigration laws were drawn up to increase the fitness of the Central American labor force by attracting a European working class. Instead, a small group of foreign entrepreneurs entered the region and became an arrogant class of merchants and planters.

With the demise or replacement of other export products, the Central American economies became increasingly focused on the production of coffee. Central America's rich volcanic soil and tropical climate gave many countries in the region a comparative advantage in coffee production. Legislation favoring export groups and the entrance of foreign capital increased the flow of raw materials out of the country and augmented a dependence on foreign markets and capital. The explosion of demand for coffee created fortunes for the lucky few in Central America, but also led to the dangerous boom-and-bust cycles that overdependence on a single export commodity can produce. In their drive for economic prosperity, the Liberals had taken the quick route of reliance on the production of export commodities. They did not learn the lesson being taught in the more advanced countries of the period, that general economic improvement depended on the growth of a larger internal market and a rise in the level of daily wages.

With the ascendancy of the Liberals, one landed oligarchy had given way to another dedicated to a variation on the same traditional values. The new elites shared the advantages of modern civilization with foreign investors but not with the majority of their compatriots. As the preeminent historian of the region has concluded, "...The oligarchies had turned over control of their countries in large measure to foreign planters, merchants, financiers, diplomats, and, in the case of Nicaragua at least, even to foreign armed forces...[The new Liberal oligarchy], based principally on producing and selling coffee to the wealthy nations, had political control, but it was a control that depended upon and had to be shared with the foreign interests which increasingly came to be typified by the great banana company." [Ralph Lee Woodward, Jr. *Central America, A Nation Divided* (New York: Oxford University Press, 1976), pp. 175-176.]

SAM THE BANANA MAN

There is perhaps no better symbol of the best and the worst of U.S. relations with Central America than the United Fruit Company (UFCO). Known as the "octopus" by its critics, for its ability to penetrate its business tentacles into every aspect of Central American politics and economics, UFCO was a dominant factor in many Central American countries for decades.

The history of United Fruit begins in 1870 when Captain Lorenzo Dow Baker of Wellfleet, Massachusetts, landed his schooner *Telegraph* in Jamaica and noticed the popularity of bananas in local markets. With the fruit largely unknown in the United States, Baker bought some green bananas and sold them eleven days later to curious vendors in Jersey City for a handsome profit.

Soon Baker, together with other investors, had established a regular trade in bananas between his home port of Boston and Jamaica, Cuba, and Santo Domingo. This Boston Fruit Company succeeded so well that the search began for new sources of supply that could produce bananas on a more sustained basis. That source was found in the person of Minor Keith, a Brooklyn-born entrepeneur who had been building railroads in Central America and exporting bananas to New Orleans and other ports to improve his cash flow. A deal was struck, and on March 13, 1899, Boston Fruit and Keith's enterprises became the United Fruit Company.

UFCO began with considerable assets, including 112 miles of railroad in Central America and 212,394 acres of land scattered throughout the Caribbean and Central America. Following a great tradition for foreign investors in Central America, UFCO became heavily involved in local politics, obtaining concessions to vast quantities of land and to monopolies of trade and transport that local corrupt rulers were only too happy to concede for the right price.

Among the shrewdest operators in this environment was Samuel Zemurray, the son of Russian peasants who became a powerful competitor of UFCO in Guatemala and Honduras until he was bought out and eventually named managing director of the entire corporation. *Bitter Fruit*, Schlesinger and Kinzer's story of the involvement of UFCO in Guatemala's politics, describes Zemurray's entry into Central America:

> In 1905, Zemurray went to Honduras, then as now a major banana producer. His plan was to buy land, build a railroad to the coast and strike a bargain with local authorities that would grant him protection against tax increases and permission to import building materials without paying duty. He was horrified to learn that Honduran President Miguel Dávila, looking for money to bail his country out of its chronic financial morass, was already in negotiation with a New York bank. In exchange for a loan, the New Yorkers insisted on naming their own agent to control Dávila's national treasury—a common arrangement in those days.
>
> Zemurray realized that no New York banker would grant him the one-sided concessions he was seeking, so he made a deal with one of Dávila's enemies, a former Honduran leader named Manuel Bonilla, who was living in exile in the United States. Zemurray bought Bonilla a surplus navy ship, the *Hornet*, a case of rifles, a machine gun and a quantity of ammunition. He personally ferried Bonilla out of New Orleans harbor, slipping past Secret Service boats trying to prevent such expeditions, and sent the adventurers on their way. Within weeks, Honduras had had yet another revolution. When the dust cleared, Manuel Bonilla was President and "Sam the Banana Man" Zemurray was holding an agreement granting him every concession he sought. [Stephen Schlesinger and Stephen Kinzer, *Bitter Fruit* (Garden City, NY: Anchor Books, 1983), p. 68.]

In some eyes, UFCO was a benevolent and paternal force in Central America. Its workers toiled under better conditions than most other farm laborers. Housing and medical facilities were built and schools provided for the children of workers. Some argued that no Central Americans had had the initiative or foresight to see their under-developed tropical lowlands as the site for a productive specialization in bananas.

But from the Central American viewpoint, the growth of the banana trade had its liabilities as well. The export orientation of the Central

American economies, where they exported raw materials and imported finished goods, was maintained and reinforced, as was the social
structure that benefited the few at the expense of the many. Although
foreigners had been important in the coffee industry, bananas were the
business almost exclusively of the *gringos*. The suspicion would always
remain, and was often justified, that corrupt leaders had sold out the
national patrimony at a cheap price. UFCO did not invent unsavory
politics in Central America. But it contributed to them by engaging in
unscrupulous business practices that had been banished in its home
country. National pride was injured further by the racial policies of the
company's mostly southern overseers, who required that "all persons
of color... give right of way to whites and remove their hats while talking
to them." This situation of poor countries dependent on outside
markets, marked by corrupt politics and *yanqui* domination, led to the
coining of the term *banana republic*.

THE ROOSEVELT THAT CENTRAL
AMERICANS DON'T LIKE

> All that this country desires is to see the neighboring countries stable,
> orderly, and prosperous. Any country whose people conduct
> themselves well can count upon our hearty friendship. If a nation shows
> that it knows how to act with reasonable efficiency and decency in social
> and political matters, if it keeps order and pays its obligations, it need
> fear no interference from the United States. Chronic wrongdoing, or an
> impotence which results in a general loosening of the ties of civilized
> society, may in America, as elsewhere, ultimately require intervention by
> some civilized nation, and in the Western Hemisphere the adherence of
> the United States to the Monroe Doctrine may force the United States,
> however reluctantly, in flagrant cases of such wrongdoing or impotence,
> to the exercise of an international police power.
>
> —The Roosevelt Corollary to the Monroe Doctrine, 1904.

The symbolic date marking the ascendancy of U.S. influence over the
Spanish and British in Latin America is probably April 20, 1898, when
the U.S. Congress ordered Spain to relinquish its authority and government in the island of Cuba, an act that led to the Spanish-American
War and brought Theodore Roosevelt to public attention as one of the
"Rough Riders" who stormed San Juan Hill. Spain's loss of its final
colony in the Americas produced a probing reexamination by intellectuals in its own society. But Spain's decline had been evident for
more than a century, and it was really the British who had constituted
the competition to U.S. influence in the region. With the dawn of the
twentieth century, British and other European trade with and in-

vestments in Latin America began to decline and those of the United States dramatically increased, establishing a pattern that endured for the next sixty years. The "Colossus of the North," as the United States had become known in Latin America, would be the dominant power in Latin America for most of the twentieth century.

The initial years after the Spanish-American War were a period that is almost universally denounced by Latin Americans. Phrases used by North Americans to characterize the period—the Big Stick, Gunboat Diplomacy, Dollar Diplomacy—give some flavor of the attitudes prevailing at that time.

The United States' self-image portrays its relations with Latin America as, in large part, differing from those between great powers and weak ones because of the unique benevolence of U.S. policies. Yet for even the staunchest defenders of the good intentions of the United States in Latin America, the first third of the twentieth century represents a low point for U.S. policy.

Two examples of U.S. relations with the region during that period that are relevant to today's problems are the treatment of Cuba after the Spanish-American War and the building of the Panama Canal. In the case of Cuba, questions about the good intentions of the United States in backing the Cuban struggle for independence were raised when the Platt Amendment was incorporated into the Cuban constitution in the early twentieth century. The amendment, named for the chairman of the Senate Foreign Relations Committee, dictated a series of terms to Cuba that severely limited her independence, until the amendment was withdrawn in 1934. Under the amendment Cuba was required to sell or lease lands to the United States for coaling or naval stations; her power to make treaties and her capacity to contract debts were limited; and the United States was given the right to intervene when it determined that Cuban independence was threatened or that law and order were not being maintained. In addition, the United States received the right to occupy a part of the island's territory (Guantanamo) in perpetuity. The Platt Amendment became a rallying cry for Cuban nationalists.

The building of the Panama Canal profoundly affected the future of Central America. From the time of Simón Bolívar, Latin Americans had speculated about the feasibility of a canal across the isthmus that would make the region, in Bolívar's words, "the capital of the world." Between 1878 and 1890, Ferdinand de Lesseps, the Frenchman who had constructed the Suez Canal, attempted to duplicate his feat across Panama, then a province of Colombia. Devastating tropical diseases and overwhelming engineering problems finally forced him to abandon the project, but the dream lived on.

Initial U.S. interest in a canal had centered on Nicaragua, and studies recommended that route as preferable. But the holders of the original French concession were desperate to recoup their losses on de Lesseps' earlier failure and lobbied the U.S. Congress hard to negotiate an agreement with the French canal company and the Colombian government. One clever ploy designed to discredit the alternate route through Nicaragua was to distribute postage stamps that pictured a "typical" Nicaraguan landscape: a jungle dominated by an active volcano. Clearly, it was argued, canals and volcanos do not mix. The promoters of the Panama route were also not above bribing members of the Republican party to switch their vote away from support for the Nicaraguan route.

Negotiations with the Colombian government over the canal during 1903 proved difficult. An initial treaty signed by the Colombian Ambassador in Washington was rejected by the government in Bogotá. Colombia was at this time experiencing another of its periodic domestic upheavals and it would be difficult to characterize the government in power as representative. But there does seem to have been widespread public resentment of the U.S. terms of a $10 million, ninety-nine year lease and annual payments of $250,000. Roosevelt grew impatient and wrote at the time, "I do not think the Bogotá lot of jack rabbits should be allowed permanently to bar one of the future highways of civilization."

The solution to the difficulties with the Colombians lay in the long tradition of rebelliousness displayed by the province of Panama itself. The United States had, in fact, helped to put down earlier uprisings against the Colombians in the province. Now the United States permitted Phillipe Bunau-Varilla, chief engineer of the de Lesseps project and an organizer of the new company holding rights to the canal concession, to instigate, finance, and direct a revolt by the Panamanians. With the help of the U.S. Navy and bribes paid to the Colombian officers who were supposed to crush the rebellion, Panama won its independence in 1903.

In a decision they were later to regret, the Panamanians entrusted negotiations over a canal concession to the same Bunau-Varilla. Desperate to work out an agreement before his company's rights to the concession expired, he agreed to a treaty that would pay the same amount that had been offered to Colombia, $10 million and an annual $250,000 payment, but for the *perpetual* use, occupation, and control of a ten-mile wide canal zone through Panama in which the United States would exercise rights "as if it were sovereign of the territory." The new Panamanian government protested the terms of the treaty but ultimately accepted it, fearing that the United States might either seize the canal with no compensation or build one in Nicaragua instead.

While Teddy Roosevelt was to proudly proclaim, "I took the canal," relations between Panama and the United States remained difficult for years, until a new treaty was negotiated in the late 1970s that will eventually turn control of the canal over to Panama by the twenty-first century. A U.S. Senator seemed to recapture the spirit of Teddy Roosevelt's approach to Central America during debate of the 1977 treaty when he argued against turning the canal over to Panama because "we stole it fair and square."

In arguing against the Panama Canal treaties in 1976, soon-to-be-President Ronald Reagan often pointed out the engineering and health-care marvel that the United States had wrought in constructing the canal on time and on budget and in defeating the tropical diseases that had decimated the ranks of workers on previous construction projects in the jungle. There is no question that the canal, with its intricate system of locks and channels, constituted a tremendous human achievement in its day and still does even now. The United States did what others had failed to do and opened a passage to trade that benefited not only the United States, but the rest of the world.

These arguments missed the point, however, that for most Panamanians the method by which the Canal Zone was obtained and the maintenance of a foreign presence and lifestyle within their borders constituted an affront to their national dignity. Even fellow conservatives such as William F. Buckley, Jr., argued against Mr. Reagan that reaching an agreement with Panama over the canal was more likely to preserve its status as a free waterway open to the world and to retain Panama as a friendly neighbor of the United States. Like much of the rest of Central America, Panama is struggling to become politically stable. A weak civilian president, elected in 1984, has been forced out of office by the military in 1985. But, so far, Panama's domestic conflicts have not involved outside powers, and most observers credit the Panama Canal Treaties with having given the United States one less headache in the region.

Theodore Roosevelt's high-handed methods for obtaining the canal took advantage of Central America's inability to establish stable and representative governments and followed a pattern that had been established even before the U.S. became a major actor in the region. His actions ushered in a period of nearly thirty years in which the United States would be more actively involved in the day-to-day affairs of Central America than at any other time—until the present. That active involvement would mean that in the future the United States would not only be taking advantage of Central America's weaknesses but would be held partially responsible for promoting and perpetuating them.

"AFTER FIFTY YEARS, SANDINO LIVES AGAIN"

Traveling around Nicaragua in 1984 a visitor encountered numerous silhouettes of a man dressed in a cowboy hat with trousers tucked in knee-high boots. The slogan below the silhouette said it all, *A 50 Años, Sandino Vive* (After Fifty Years, Sandino Lives Again). The figure is that of Augusto Sandino, who became a hero for many Nicaraguans by fighting and eluding U.S. Marines during the nearly twenty-year occupation of Nicaragua by the United States after 1912. His struggle and death in 1934 inspired a revolution that preoccupies the United States today because of the revolution's ties to Cuba and the Soviet Union. The story of Sandino and of U.S. involvement in Nicaragua in the first third of the twentieth century is a rather extreme example of U.S.-Central American relations, but an illustrative one.

The Panama Canal was the most visible symbol of U.S. economic and political involvement in Central American affairs. The increased stake of the United States in the region heightened its sensitivity to the "chronic wrongdoing" that had afflicted Central American politics since independence and encouraged the United States to exercise the "international police power" of which Roosevelt had spoken in his famous corollary. The occasion of "chronic wrongdoing" in Nicaragua was a rather typical squabble between Conservatives who were out of power in Nicaragua and the Liberals who had another in their series of dictators in the presidency. Liberal President Zelaya had alienated some of his Conservative countrymen with attacks on the church and had upset foreign businessmen by increasing taxes. When a revolt by Conservatives, assisted financially by North American and other foreign interests, broke out in 1909 and led to the death of two U.S. citizens who were fighting with the rebels, the United States entered civil war on the side of the Conservatives. With U.S. military help, the Conservatives gained power and ultimately installed as president Adolfo Díaz, a former employee of a U.S. mining concession in Nicaragua. At one point some 2,000 U.S. Marines occupied strategic positions in Nicaragua to maintain Díaz and the Conservatives in power. A treaty conferring a virtual protectorate status on Nicaragua was signed, and a smaller contingent of Marines remained from 1912 until 1925, supervising elections and discouraging Liberal challenges to the Conservatives. Following the election of a Conservative president in 1925, the Marines withdrew, but new rebellions broke out almost immediately.

Bitter warfare between the Liberals and Conservatives, involving a growing number of U.S. troops and aircraft, continued for three years until the Liberal general agreed to a truce. Feeling the Liberal cause had been betrayed, Augusto Cesar Sandino, the son of a small landholder and an Indian peasant, chose to fight on. He and his ragged troops were defeated in battle after battle until they adopted the hit-and-run tactics we know today as guerrilla warfare. He eluded the U.S. Marines and the Nicaraguan National Guard, which the United States was training to take over military supervision of the country. Only the election, in 1932, of a Liberal president who had campaigned on a platform of U.S. withdrawal could persuade Sandino to give up his fight against the "Yankee imperialists." In January 1933 the last U.S. troops left Nicaragua. But long-term damage had been done. Anastasio Somoza, the bilingual head of the National Guard and lover of the United States Ambassador's wife, had Sandino assassinated as he was leaving the National Palace on the night of February 21, 1934. By 1936, Somoza had removed the elected Liberal president and installed himself as the head of a political dynasty that ruled Nicaragua for the next forty years.

Although denounced by the United States as a bandit, Sandino was in the eyes of many a nationalist fed up with the failures of the ruling political elites and their willingness to invite foreign intervention to bolster the position of one side or the other. In death he became a hero, and thirty years later, the inspiration to young Nicaraguans who would take up arms against the son of the original Somoza. In 1979 the Sandinista National Liberation Front defeated Somoza and made Sandino live again after fifty years. The Sandinista anthem denounces the Yankee as the "enemy of humanity."

THE OLD SYSTEM BEGINS TO BREAK DOWN

The intervention of the United States in Nicaragua was more far-reaching than those in other Central American countries, but it reflected an increasing preoccupation on the part of the United States with the region. Unfortunately for the United States, this heightened concern for stability in the area coincided with a period of great change in the domestic politics of the countries. New social groups emerged to challenge the traditional elites for a share of power, and provocative ideas such as nationalism and socialism made themselves felt in intellectual circles. At a time when many Central Americans were desperate for change to better their lives, U.S. policy often came to be equated with support for the status quo. This was a legacy that has burdened U.S. policies in the region until the present.

The efforts of the Liberals to modernize and develop their societies in the late nineteenth and early twentieth centuries had not achieved the kind of general prosperity and progress that had been hoped for.

Rather, certain sectors of the economy and society, the better-off and urban dwellers, had advanced while the rural countryside had languished in a poverty dominated by the values and institutions of a century before. Rural inhabitants were lured to the cities by the often-unfulfilled promise of employment and economic advancement, and they formed pockets of poverty that would eventually become huge slums around the capitals and other large cities. Achievements in the control of epidemic diseases and other improvements in medical care led to a drop in infant mortality rates and dramatic increase in the population.

In these expanding cities, a much more significant middle class began to emerge. But the middle class was not dominant in most Central American countries as it was in the United States. Weak and dependent, the Central American middle class aped their upper-class compatriots, who set the tone for society and continued to monopolize political life. The refusal of the traditional elites to make way for the middle class and other new groups in the political arena eventually led to revolutionary turmoil. Only in Costa Rica, always an exception to the Central American rule, was such turmoil avoided (as we shall see below).

Insignificant numerically but important because of their concentration in the centers of political power, workers organized themselves into unions that often had a radical cast of Marxism or socialism. Examples and pressure from outside the region led to legislation that, formally at least, recognized minimum labor rights such as the forty-eight hour week, overtime pay, worker's compensation, and so on.

The emphasis of the Liberals on education had increased the impact of university students and intellectuals on the political system. The upper class still sent their children abroad to be educated, but national universities in Central America became middle-class institutions and accelerated the aspirations of this group. This educated elite experimented with a range of ideologies from communism to fascism, but all focused increasingly on the need for greater nationalism. Conscious of their status as underdeveloped nations, Central Americans' nationalism was often rooted in resentment, fear, frustration, and a sense of inferiority. It was frequently violent and angry, and it had a strong impact on the rest of the population.

COSTA RICA, ALWAYS THE EXCEPTION

The generalizations that have been made about Central America throughout this chapter cannot do justice to the richness and complexity of the individual countries' histories. But the story of Costa

Rica's development is especially different from that of the rest of Central America.

In the 1980s, Costa Rica is far from a paradise and has severe economic and social strains. But it feels like a breath of fresh air after being in the rest of Central America. While the recent history of much of the region is a story of death, destruction, and dictatorship, Costa Rica has been a functioning democracy that abolished a standing army and instituted far-reaching social reforms nearly forty years ago.

Just as the origins of many of the rest of Central America's problems lie in history, so too are the reasons for Costa Rica's relative success found in her past. Despite her name, "Rich Coast," the early Spanish explorers found little of the mineral wealth in Costa Rica that attracted them to other parts of Central America. Those Spaniards who decided to settle in what was to become Costa Rica fought fierce battles with the small indigenous population and virtually eliminated them. Without mines or a subservient labor force to work plantation-style agriculture, the early colonists set up small family farms similar to those found in North America. As a result, the tiny aristocratic elite that ruled the rest of Central America never developed as fully in Costa Rica. The slight economic importance of Costa Rica to Spain and its relative isolation meant that Hispanic institutions were never as strongly imposed on Costa Rica's small population as they were on those of the other Central American countries. The country's politics, therefore, were always more egalitarian and middle class than those prevailing in the rest of Central America. The elimination of the native population allowed Costa Rica to avoid the problems caused by racial mixing and color barriers. By 1925 the population was nearly 80 percent white with a small *mestizo* group (14 percent), a tiny black population concentrated on the coasts, and an Indian group of less than 1 percent.

There were clearly differences between rich and poor. But there also developed an agrarian middle sector—virtually unknown in the rest of Central America—based on family-sized farms that allowed a wider distribution of wealth. No landless subclass dominated the countryside. The agrarian middle sector and a relatively literate and democratically oriented urban population placed checks on foreign domination of the economic life of the country. Costa Rica specialized in both coffee and bananas, as did the rest of Central America. But an elected leadership, more responsive to popular needs, made foreign participation in the economy more a partnership than a case of exploitation. Taxes were levied on UFCO's operations and requirements made that railroads be constructed and other benefits bestowed on the state in return for concessions on banana lands.

When the Western capitalist economy collapsed in 1929 and desperation drove popular forces to consider radical alternatives such as communism and fascism, strong-arm dictators seized power in every Central American country except Costa Rica. Even in Costa Rica there were riots, worker uprisings, and suspension of constitutional guarantees. But unlike the other countries, Costa Rica produced political parties that promised reform and offered effective alternatives to communism as a way to resolve social conflict. In the rest of Central America, where powerful oligarchies feared the masses and where tiny middle classes had no control over the political system, right-wing dictatorships were the response to the political and economic crises of the 1930s.

DEPRESSION AND REPRESSION

Throughout Latin America, the decline of export markets and the fall in prices because of the world depression of the 1930s produced challenges to the traditional methods of politics. This happened in Central America as well. The reaction of the traditional elites was to find a strongman who could hold the forces of change in check at least for a while. Whether it was General Jorge Ubico in Guatemala (1930-1944), General Maximiliano Hernández Martínez in El Salvador (1931-1944), Anastasio Somoza in Nicaragua (1936-1956), or Tiburcio Carías Andino in Honduras (1932-1949), the methods of power were strikingly similar: censorship of the press, exile or jail for the opposition, pervasive police control, special privileges for the prominent coffee producers, and generous treatment of the interests of foreign corporations.

The reaction against protest took monstrous proportions in some cases. In El Salvador a peasant uprising in January 1932 was led by Augusto Farabundo Martí, head of the fledgling Communist party. Several landlords were murdered, and the movement threatened to establish a collective-based government. The army defeated the poorly equipped band of Indian rebels and then began a systematic slaughter of the Indian population in the rebel region. Between 10,000 and 40,000 peasants died in the army's action. Today in El Salvador, one of the death squads is named in honor of General Hernández and his response to challenges from the left. The coalition of guerrilla groups, the Farabundo Martí Liberation Front (FMLN), takes its name from the fallen Communist leader.

Somoza's system of control in Nicaragua was perhaps the most sophisticated. Power was concentrated in his own hands and those of his political family. Opposition—particularly of the left—was ruthlessly repressed, but he was kept in power by more than the U.S.-trained

National Guard. His emphasis on material progress—at least for the privileged few—helped to create the strongest and most durable family dynasty in Central American history. He and, after his assassination, his family controlled nearly every facet of Nicaraguan economic life: land, industry, banking, transportation, and commerce. It was estimated that by 1970 they owned more than half the agricultural production of the republic and had vast financial resources invested in industry, mining, and commerce in and outside Nicaragua.

Somoza continued his earlier close association with the "Yankees" who had helped place him in power. He received increasing amounts of economic and military assistance and acknowledged the importance of the United States to his regime by locating the U.S. embassy virtually on the grounds of the presidential palace. As Franklin Roosevelt said of Somoza, "He's a son of a bitch, but he's ours."

FRANKLIN DELANO ROOSEVELT AND THE GOOD NEIGHBOR POLICY

The period of blatant intervention by the United States during the first third of the twentieth century eventually produced a strong reaction throughout Latin America. Repeatedly in inter-American conferences during the period, Latin American critics of U.S. policy in the region raised the issue of nonintervention in the internal and external affairs of the Latin American republics. An active participant in two earlier interventions by President Wilson in Mexico and Haiti, Roosevelt argued that a change was needed in U.S.-Latin American relations. While campaigning for governor of New York in 1928, he wrote an article for *Foreign Affairs* magazine that criticized U.S. interventions in the Caribbean region and demanded the renunciation "for all time" of "arbitrary intervention in the home affairs of our neighbors." As president, he pledged the United States to pursue the policy of a good neighbor in her international relations.

Roosevelt's good intentions were reinforced by the increasing problems in Europe during the 1930s. Several conflicts between nationalistic governments and U.S. businesses were resolved in Latin America's favor, most notably the nationalization of the oil industry in Mexico in 1938. As war clouds increased in Europe, Roosevelt became more concerned about the loyalty of the Mexican government than about the economic interests of the large corporations and forced accommodation on companies used to unquestioning defense of their prerogatives.

Critics of U.S. policy toward Latin America question the degree to which Roosevelt actually changed U.S. behavior toward the region. But in Central America the popular perception is that Roosevelt's Good Neighbor Policy was successful. The record of that success remains in the schools, hospitals, and roads named after the president or the first lady and in the positive response his memory evokes among the common people.

THE WAR AND ITS AFTERMATH: REFORM OR REVOLUTION?

The wartime partnership between the United States and Latin America lasted about as long as that between the United States and the Soviet Union. Scarcity produced by the war years was a boon to the export economies of Central America, but increased prosperity only caused greater discontent with the repressive dictatorships that had ruled much of Central America since the Great Depression. In rapid succession, the dictators of Guatemala (1944), El Salvador (1944), and Honduras (1948) were overthrown, and even Somoza in Nicaragua was forced to juggle a series of puppet presidents to maintain his grip on power.

New ideas about social change and economic development pervaded the postwar world. Diverse social groups such as university professors and students, government officials, small businessmen and urban artisans, and some elements of the professional military tentatively supported social reforms. These reforms included minimal social security legislation providing medical assistance and unemployment compensation, the right to unionize, and a labor code. In the economic sphere, there was agreement on a certain level of state control of the banking and credit industries, plans for agricultural reform, and a policy of economic diversification. As regards politics, reinforcing constitutional, representative democracy and the principle of electoral politics—one, but not the only route to power in Central America—were priorities. Finally, taxation of the banana companies, as one of a series of nationalist measures, completed the picture of the basic reform program.

The relative success or failure of these reform programs depended on several factors. One was the ability of the dominant class to move against the reforms. The traditional elites saw any concession on reformist issues as opening the road to social revolution and, in the Cold War atmosphere that came to dominate the period, they adopted an anticommunist ideology that branded as "red" even the most modest changes. As the case of Costa Rica illustrates, a second factor determining the possibilities for reform was the relative importance of the middle sectors and the opportunity they had to play a political role supportive of reform. A final factor was the prevailing international context and in particular the policy of the United States. As events in Guatemala in the 1950s demonstrated, the ability of the United States to distinguish between reform and revolution had profound implications for the future of reformist projects in Central America.

A HARVEST OF BITTER FRUIT

From October 1944 to June 1954, Guatemala lived out a reformist drama. Depending on your perspective, the U.S.-organized invasion that ended this social experiment in 1954 was either the first successful rebuff to communist designs on the hemisphere or a tragic misreading of the reformist impulse in Central America that would lead to the more troublesome conflicts of the 1980s in El Salvador and Nicaragua.

Ubico's long dictatorship finally ended in mid-1944. Elections in December brought Dr. Juan José Arévalo, an exiled educator and philosopher, to power. An intellectual and idealistic man, Dr. Arévalo promulgated a vague doctrine of "spiritual socialism," which seemed to offer the hope of change without committing the country to a revolutionary program. Elected by a broad front that won over 85 percent of the vote, Arévalo moved to implement a reformist program. His government established social security, founded a Native People's Institute for Guatemala's majority Indian population, and developed health programs, a labor code, and a state organization devoted to the promotion of economic development.

The fall of Ubico had brought back many political exiles who carried with them some of the Marxist and leftist ideas to which they had been exposed in exile. They, together with foreigners attracted to the possibility for social change, sought to develop a Marxist ideology among Guatemalan workers and political leaders.

The appeal of communism to Guatemalan workers was not surprising. No other domestic group sought to attract their allegiance. Ignorant of the international communist movement and of the political and economic theory it espoused, the average worker knew that he had been economically and socially exploited and oppressed and prohibited from organizing effectively to support his own interests. Communist intellectuals, foreign and Guatemalan, offered to the worker the possibility of advancement while no one else seemed to care.

As the election of 1950 approached, the internal political situation began to polarize. The new pro-worker legislation and the proliferation of unions provoked conflicts with the important interests of the

United Fruit Company and challenged the privileged position of the coffee producers. There were twenty-two military revolts during Arevalo's five years in the presidency. On occasion the government issued arms to workers to aid in the suppression of the military revolts.

The election of Colonel Jacobo Arbenz in 1950 began the countdown to the end of Guatemala's experiment. An agrarian reform law was passed in 1952 that affected all landowners with over 250 acres, especially United Fruit, which controlled about 550,000 acres on Guatemala's Atlantic and Pacific coasts. The expropriation of over 200,000 acres of uncultivated land held in reserve by United Fruit brought the confrontation to a head. The Guatemalan government offered $600,000 in bonds as compensation for the land, an amount based on UFCO's declared tax value. As was customary among foreign companies operating in Central America, UFCO undervalued its property for tax purposes and screamed in protest to the U.S. government when this understated value was used as the basis for compensation. The United States presented, on behalf of UFCO, a demand for over $16 million in compensation.

UFCO was well positioned in Washington during the Eisenhower administration. Secretary of State John Foster Dulles had done legal work for clients connected to UFCO, as had his brother, Allen Dulles, head of the CIA. John Moors Cabot, assistant secretary of state for inter-American affairs, had family holdings in UFCO, and his brother Thomas had served as president of the corporation in 1948. United Nations Ambassador Henry Cabot Lodge was also a stockholder and had defended UFCO's interests many times as the senator from Massachusetts.

For many in and outside Guatemala, the attack on United Fruit was proof positive that Guatemala was falling into communist hands. The CIA was authorized to mount operation *El Diablo* (the Devil) to remove Arbenz and the purported communist threat. A complex series of maneuvers ensued, involving the training of an exile army in Honduras led by two former Guatemalan officers opposed to the reforms, the obtaining of international support, CIA aerial bombings to intimidate Arbenz supporters, and the condemnation of an arms shipment from Czechoslovakia (the United States had previously blocked Guatemalan arms purchases from noncommunist countries). After losing the support of the military and refusing to call out the unions to battle the invaders, Arbenz resigned on June 27, 1954, seven days after the CIA army had entered Guatemalan territory. One of the first acts of the new leader of Guatemala, Castillo Armas, was to return the expropriated property to United Fruit.

The "lessons" of Guatemala were different for each of the parties involved. For the right in Guatemala and in the United States, a blow had been struck against the international communist conspiracy and a country "liberated" from communist rule in a way that Eastern Europe apparently could not be. Moderates thought the coup a tragic misreading of nationalist aspirations in Central America. A modest reform program—much less far-reaching than that promoted by the United States in El Salvador in the 1980s—had been branded as communism and prevented from making those basic changes that had a possibility of preventing a truly explosive situation. The left drew the conclusion that no middle road was possible and that U.S. imperialism would oppose any reform in Latin America that threatened the interests of its large corporations. Ernesto "Che" Guevara, the Argentine revolutionary who later came to power with Fidel Castro in Cuba, watched the U.S.-engineered coup from a post in the Guatemalan agrarian reform institute. He viewed as key the betrayal of Arbenz by the traditional armed forces and took steps to eliminate the army as a threat to Cuba's revolution after 1959.

Since the 1950s the specter of Soviet intervention in Latin America has haunted U.S. policy toward the region. Cynical Latin Americans, mindful of the Monroe Doctrine, have argued that the supposed communist threat was just the latest in a series of convenient pretexts that the United States has used for maintaining its position of dominace. They have pointed out that the poverty, disease, and exploitation that the Central American elites have helped to create cannot be overcome by appeals to democratic slogans. Instead a frontal assault on the privileges and power that have been amassed in the hands of the few would be required. If the United States would not help to change this situation, weren't patriots justified in seeking help from outside powers who, for their own strategic reasons, were interested in seeing the status quo altered?

Perhaps the dilemma for U.S. policy was best presented by President John F. Kennedy who coined the axiom, "Those who make peaceful change impossible make violent change inevitable." Complacent about Central America for decades, the United States was unprepared to deal with the wave of social change that swept through the Third World in the postwar period. Central America's ruling groups were ready to resist change with every means at their disposal. When the inevitable confrontation came, which side would the United States choose?

TO THE CONTEMPORARY CRISIS

The decades of the 1960s and 1970s in Central America saw the continued emergence of new social groups and political actors. The middle class, historically a small minority in Central American politics, had grown larger and become more diverse. Its challenge to the traditional oligarchic structure forced the ruling elites to defend themselves by seeking new allies in the military and through anticommunist appeals to the United States. In some cases, the working class and the peasantry developed mass organizations that were also capable of confronting the traditional power structure. Explosive combinations were created when disaffected elements of the middle class, following the Cuban model, linked up with mass-based organizations of peasants or workers.

The military as an institution changed dramatically over the course of the twentieth century. In the first third of the century, it developed into one of the few semimeritocratic institutions in Central America. The creation of military schools with entrance by examination opened a new route to social status for those from the lower middle class. Now the son of a poor schoolteacher, minor government official, or small shopowner could aspire to achieve real power, even the presidency of his country, and to appropriate through corruption the wealth that political power made possible.

The military ranks did not remain a monolith. They too were affected by the currents of social change swirling through society at large. Some elements, often the younger officers who saw their possibilities of advancement blocked by a top-heavy senior officer corps, forged links with progressive civilians and attempted to institute reforms to preempt more drastic revolutionary change. These progressive coups rarely endured, however, because of the unwillingness of the military to institutionalize reform through civilian and popularly based political structures.

The more common pattern was for the military to strike a deal with the old landholding oligarchies to defend their interests by force and repression. In return for their protection, the military were allowed to take a cut of the economic pie. This arrangement endured in many of the Central American countries for much of the 1960s and 1970s. But it began to break down under the pressure of economic shocks delivered to the region in the 1970s and the continued emergence of new challenges to the status quo.

A significant new actor on the Central American scene during the 1970s was a progressive Catholic church. From Spanish colonial times on, the church had generally been viewed as an ally of the rich and powerful. Its response to the deprivation of most of its flock was to counsel patience and comfort in the consolation of a heavenly reward for those who had suffered in this life. Linked to the elite by interest as well as birthright, the Catholic church had played, with rare exceptions, a role consistently supportive of the status quo.

In the 1960s and 1970s, new forces began to stir in the church. Inspired by the doctrines of renewal developed by the Second Vatican

Council (1962-1965), many in the Latin American church sought to break the long-standing association of the Catholic Church with the interests of the powerful. First in Medellín, Colombia in 1968, and later in 1979 in Puebla, Mexico, Roman Catholic bishops of Latin America met to examine critically the role of the church in their societies. In these meetings, they condemned the institutionalized violence of the status quo and indicted those with "the greater share of wealth and power" who "jealously retain their privileges thus provoking 'explosive revolutions of despair.'" In dramatic statements, they took it upon themselves to defend the rights of the poor and oppressed and to encourage efforts by the poor to develop their own grassroots organizations. Criticizing both capitalism and communism, their pronouncements often seemed to support a kind of benign socialism that would recognize the communal nature of human beings while not violating basic rights of liberty and religious freedom. Some within the church spoke of the development of a "Christian Marxism" and a "theology of liberation." A few prominent priests went to the hills to join guerrilla struggles. In Nicaragua in the late 1970s, the church was a powerful force in helping to overthrow the Somoza dynasty. El Salvador's Archbishop Romero, before his assassination by the right in 1980, was also an eloquent critic of the power structure and a spokesperson for the poor and the politically repressed.

In the 1980s, reaction to these liberalizing trends in the church set in. More conservative bishops, who had always been uncomfortable with the idea of "liberation theology," reasserted the church hierarchy's prerogatives. The Polish pope, John Paul II, who had direct experience with the conflicts between the church and a communist state, cautioned against too political a stance for priests. In Nicaragua, church authorities clashed with the Sandinista leadership and splits developed between the church hierarchy, increasingly opposed to the Sandinistas, and the so-called popular church of priests and nuns who worked with the poor and even occupied cabinet positions in the Sandinista government.

Despite these signs of internal turmoil, the church in the mid-1980s was clearly not the conservative institution it had been only fifteen or twenty years before. Together with other changes in Central American society, the new Catholic Church was a powerful indicator that the old order would come under increasing attack.

That old order had in fact exhausted itself by the early 1960s. One of the surest signs of its demise was the increasing irrelevance of the old party labels of Liberal and Conservative. A proliferation of new parties and movements emerged over the course of the 1960s and 1970s, sometimes representing factions of the old parties, but often introducing new strains into the political mix. The new parties frequently drew their inspiration from Western Europe, not the United States. Examples included the Christian Democrats, who won the presidency of El Salvador in 1972 and 1984 and of Guatemala in 1985, and were also important in other Central American countries. They tried to combine the region's tradition of Catholicism with progressive social policies that were, nevertheless, staunchly anticommunist. Various Social Democratic tendencies emerged that were also noncommunist but even more disposed than the Christian Democrats to promote state intervention in civil society. Noncommunist socialist parties developed, again inspired by European traditions. Each of these political formations was strengthened by regional and international links with similar parties in Latin America and in Europe.

On the right, various groupings developed that sought to defend traditional interests through the new methods of popular appeals and the ballot box. Among the more interesting experiments were attempts to imitate the Mexican single-party state by dominating the political system while tolerating a feeble opposition. None of the right-wing parties was able, however, to maintain itself in power for long without the active collaboration of the military.

Another group that entered Central American politics with a vengeance in the 1960s was leftist guerrillas. Largely inspired by the perceived success of armed struggle in Cuba, groups of students, intellectuals, and other disaffected members of the middle class took to the hills (or jungles) and attempted to recruit peasants to the cause of revolution. Some of these revolutionaries were moderates who had despaired of peaceful attempts to achieve social change. Others were members of socialist or communist parties who grew disillusioned with the willingness of their parties' leadership to work within the system.

Cuban-inspired guerrilla movements met with spectacular failures in most of Latin America and helped to precipitate, in some cases, the brutal authoritarian regimes of the 1960s and 1970s. In a pattern that would be repeated later in other Central American countries, the guerrillas had some success in that country where reformist approaches had been defeated: Guatemala. Guerrilla movements led by rebellious army officers began in Guatemala in the late 1950s and continued with intermittent success throughout the 1960s and 1970s. The guerrillas' actions produced the now classic response: death squads—semiofficial assassination teams operating above the law—and U.S. counterinsurgency advisers. After 1966, Guatemala unleashed a withering attack on the "forces of subversion." More than 30,000 people were tortured or assassinated. In the ferocious warfare, much of the moderate center as well as the left was eliminated. During the 1980s, when the guerrillas again began to make inroads in the Indian population, a savage war was mounted that adopted the old North

American slogan, "The only good Indian is a dead Indian." Cut off from U.S. aid because of disputes over human-rights abuses during the Carter administration, Guatemala's military adopted tactics that probably violated all the conventions of modern warfare but that did succeed in pacifying the countryside.

In Nicaragua, guerrilla bands named for the fallen patriot Augusto Sandino began operations against the Somozas in the 1960s. They were largely unsuccessful until "Tachito" Somoza, son of the first dictator, scandalized even his supporters by misappropriating disaster-relief aid for the devastating 1972 earthquake that virtually destroyed the capital, Managua. Castro's Cuba also played a role in the guerrillas' success by serving as a training base, by forging coalitions among the conflicting guerrilla groups, and by providing direct military assistance in the final decisive months. The Sandinistas came to power in 1979 at the head of a broad front of anti-Somoza opposition groups after a civil war that cost 40,000 lives.

The other site of relative success by the guerrillas was El Salvador. In 1979, another in a series of reformist military coups provoked a civil war that has taken an estimated 50,000 lives. Guerrillas, linked politically to democratic-minded politicians who had abandoned hope for peaceful reform, were able by the mid-1980s to occupy one-fourth of the national territory. However, government forces, with massive U.S. assistance, gradually forced a stalemate in the war and opened the possibility of a military victory over the guerrillas by the late 1980s.

The Soviet Union opposed Castro's armed-struggle strategy for much of the 1960s and 1970s as risky and unproductive. It preferred to influence events through the conventional approach of pro-Moscow communist parties. Some analysts believe, however, that the Sandinistas' success has persuaded the Soviet Union of the correctness of Cuba's strategy. They expect that the Soviet Union and Cuba will become more active on the Central American political stage in the 1980s.

THE SIMMERING POT OF CENTRAL AMERICA

The crisis now gripping Central America has multiple dimensions. One underlying cause of the escalation of conflict during the 1970s was the severe economic contraction that hit the Third World in general and especially the small Central American countries after the oil shocks of 1973 and 1979. Escalating oil costs and declining prices for Central America's exports impoverished the region and forced the countries to accumulate huge external debts to maintain prior standards of living.

The dream of Central America's reunification was reborn in the 1960s with the establishment of a Central American Common Market that promised to improve economic conditions by expanding the size of each country's potential market. Industrialization to substitute for imports was intended to diversify Central America away from its traditional dependence on exports of coffee, bananas, and cotton. Central America was following the advice given to most other developing countries that continued reliance on traditional exports would doom their economies to chronic poverty. Demand for coffee, bananas, or other tropical exports did not rise as quickly as incomes in the rich countries. To buy crucial imports, the Central American countries had to export larger and larger amounts of their products at the same or reduced prices. Import substitution, it was argued, would lessen costly imports and begin a process of industrialization that would allow the countries to produce new exports. The Common Market would complement this process by lowering tariff barriers between the countries and expanding the potential market size beyond each country's own relatively small population. Foreign aid, principally from the United States, and foreign investment added the necessary infusion of capital to launch the process.

The Common Market began auspiciously. Trade within the region multiplied sevenfold between 1961 and 1968. But over time, market forces tended to accentuate rather than lessen differences among the countries. Guatemala and El Salvador, the countries with greater populations and lower salaries, benefited disproportionately from the Common Market, while Nicaragua, Costa Rica, and, especially, Honduras grew increasingly resentful of the effects of the market on their economies. The so-called Soccer War between El Salvador and Honduras in 1969, which began with violence at a soccer match and was fueled by the large number of Salvadoran immigrants in Honduras, made maintenance of the market more difficult. Honduras eventually withdrew from the market in 1971.

By the end of the 1970s, the alternative model of development offered by the Common Market appeared to have failed. As in the rest of Latin America, import-substitution industrialization proved to be a dead end. Fewer finished goods were imported, but large amounts of raw materials and intermediate products still needed to be imported for the industrialization process. The small market size and inefficiencies of production made Central American industrial products expensive and unable to compete with cheaper goods made elsewhere unless their producers were protected by high tariffs. Before long, the Central American businessmen found themselves in the familiar situation of producing inferior goods at uncompetitive prices. They lobbied governments to protect them in their domestic markets and were unable to export to help the countries earn valuable foreign exchange. This situation continued until the oil shock of 1973, when escalating oil prices created balance-of-payments crises in all the Central American countries.

This sequence of events proved to be an explosive combination. The import-substitution industrialization of the 1960s and early 1970s had produced the appearance of prosperity in urban areas, while aggravating the desperate conditions of the rural masses. Thus the unequal distribution of income became even more glaring. Urban workers and national businessmen who had profited during the import substitution years suddenly found their economic fortunes reversed in the late 1970s and sought political solutions of the left and right to preserve their economic positions. Traditional elites responded in their customary fashion by pushing the lid down tighter on a political stew near the boiling point. Indifference and neglect by the United States and the stake of Cuba and the Soviet Union in the disruption of the status quo proved to be the fatal mix. By the mid-1980s, the United States would be fighting wars—by advice and proxies—in two Central American countries and preparing a third—Honduras—as a base of supply should its own troops need to be used in the future.

THE LESSONS OF CENTRAL AMERICAN HISTORY

This one-chapter history of Central America from Columbus to Castro cannot do justice to the complex experience of that region of the world. But the brief review does illustrate basic themes that are crucial to any discussion of the contemporary Central American crisis.

1. *Political Instability.* Given Central America's origins, it is not surprising that democratic political systems modeled on the United States or Western Europe did not develop. Except for Costa Rica, none of the countries of the region seem to have that peculiar set of political, economic, and social conditions that have produced democratic governments. But even more striking is the inability of any political formula, even nondemocratic, to achieve the minimal goals of stability, economic progress, and the integration of the majority of the population into national life. Assigning historical blame is always a risky business. But Central America's political elites seem to bear responsibility for their failure to develop a vision of society that would produce a better future. Jealously guarding their short-term privileges, they have produced a situation that cannot endure indefinitely and is bound now to be influenced by actors outside their control, such as the United States, or Cuba and the Soviet Union.

2. *The Fragile Economy.* The artificiality of any division between politics and economics is reinforced by a reading of the history of Central America. Ever since the origins of Central America as a colony designed to produce wealth for Mother Spain, economics has placed limits on possible political arrangements. These tiny countries, linked so tightly to the fluctuations of the international market, are highly vulnerable. Policies adopted in Washington or at an OPEC meeting can mean the difference literally between life and death for the poorest sectors of Central America's population.

This tense economic environment makes constructive political arrangements all that much more difficult. Any attempts to democratize politics require assaults on the privileged positions of the economic elites, specifically the breaking up of large estates and the redistribution of scarce land. While widely seen as desirable politically and socially, this disruption of agricultural production often decreases absolute output because of less efficient methods or the natural tendency of the peasant to consume more of his product in his own meager diet. Unless followed up with credit facilities for seeds and fertilizers and extension services to teach proper farming methods, land reform can leave the peasants worse off than before. All this costs money that the Central American countries do not have.

3. *The Role of the United States.* Any review of the history of Central America suggests that, for better or worse, the United States has been preoccupied with that part of the world. It is the relative neglect of the area during the 1970s, not the heavy involvement of the 1980s, that seems atypical. The United States has certainly contributed to Central America's problems. The invasions and direct occupations of Central American countries early in this century produced stability but at the cost of dictatorships whose legacies are now being played out in the region.

In a perfect world, the Central American countries could work out their destinies free from outside interference. Who knows what unique combinations of political life would evolve to face the region's dilemmas? But that perfect world does not and has never existed. From their beginnings as independent states, the Central American countries have meddled in each others' affairs and have been the object of rivalries by the big powers.

The stakes in Central America in the 1980s are higher than ever. For reasons beyond its control, the region has become a test case for U.S. resolve in a global chess match with the Soviet Union. Uncertain of the role it must play in the Third World, the United States deals with Central America while attempting to reconstruct a foreign-policy consensus that was shattered by the Vietnam experience.

Central American history has some hard lessons for the United States. Traditionally linked to the status quo, the United States will be viewed with hostility by many Central Americans seeking to remake their future. The United States is the logical scapegoat for the forces of nationalism and social change. Radical movements will be likely to imitate the Sandinistas and view the Yankee as the "enemy of humanity."

Neglectful of the region for so long and content to let friendly dictators deal with Central America's glaring problems in their own style, the United States must now play catch-up. In El Salvador, it has chosen to back moderate reform, to tolerate the traditional right, and to attempt to exclude the radical left. Elsewhere in the region, the United States has been less clear about which side it is on, encouraging civilian democracies, but barely addressing the underlying social and economic tensions. In the case of Nicaragua, the Reagan administration seems certain that the Sandinistas must go, but has yet to devise a strategy to achieve that goal at acceptable political costs.

History tells us that the United States has often taken Central America for granted. In the shadow of the United States, Central America was an area of the world that could be relied on as being safe and secure for U.S. interests with little expenditure of money or manpower. That situation is now changing. The United States faces a difficult and fateful choice in Central America. It can seek to restore the isthmus to its former compliant position, with all the political and military costs that entails. Or it can try to create some new way of coexisting with its southern neighbors that places the United States on the side of social, political, and economic change; however, this alternative runs the risk that, in surrendering control of the region, the United States will be forced to deal with regimes that challenge important U.S. interests.

NOTES

[1]. A *hacienda* was a special kind of agricultural institution that developed in much of Latin America. Largely self-sufficient, it differed from a plantation in that it did not specialize in the production of a cash crop for export to external markets. *Haciendas* and plantations in Latin America contributed to the development of two other phenomena, *minifundio* and *latifundio*. *Minifundio* (literally, tiny plots) is the division of the small amounts of land available to the peasants into plots too small to be efficient or to support the families dependent on them. *Latifundio* is the corresponding problem of large, underutilized estates maintained by the aristocracy. Strictly speaking, the *hacienda* reached its greatest development in the nineteenth century, but the social

pressures created by the elite's monopolization of land existed in various forms from the earliest decades of the Spanish conquest.

 [2].   Grin'go, n.; grin'gos, [Sp., gibberish.] among Spanish-Americans, an Englishman or American; hostile and contemptuous term.
—Webster's Dictionary

 [3].   While Latin Americans in private and sometimes in public refer to citizens of the United States by the less than complimentary term *gringo*, they object when these same citizens refer to themselves as "Americans." They argue, quite rightly, that all inhabitants of the Western Hemisphere are Americans and that it is arrogant of those from North America to reserve the term to themselves. The moral is that if you don't want to be called a *gringo*, it helps to acknowledge that you're a *North* American, as we do in this book.

 [4].   Manifest Destiny: The nineteenth-century doctrine that it is the destiny of the Anglo-Saxon nations, especially of the United States, to dominate the entire Western Hemisphere.

2 Central American "Snapshots"

NICARAGUA: A REVOLUTION BESIEGED

"*Poder al Pueblo*" (Power to the People) is the chant that rises from the crowd of Sandinista militants assembled in Managua's largest movie theater, where later that night, militants and *la burguesa* (the upper social classes) alike will watch *Kramer vs. Kramer*. These militants, members of local CDSs—Committees in Defense of *Sandinismo*—have gathered to commemorate the anniversary of the death of Carlos Fonseca in 1976 at the hands of Somoza's National Guard. Fonseca, a founder in 1958 of the Sandinista National Liberation Front (FSLN), and 1930s nationalist leader César Augusto Sandino, are the Thomas Jefferson and George Washington (or Karl Marx and Vladimir Lenin) of Nicaragua.

Tomás Borge, the only living founder of the FSLN, is at fifty-five the grand old man of the revolution. A tight, energetic man dressed in the green fatigues that are the uniform of the Sandinista leadership, he eulogizes Fonseca with forceful and inspiring rhetoric. Borge is undoubtedly the best speaker the Sandinistas have, and he mesmerizes the crowd with his wit and zeal. Tomás Borge has often said, *la revolucíon no es una piñata* (the revolution does not have something for everyone). But the crowd is clearly having great fun that began with Carlos Mejía Godoy's exotic brand of revolutionary lyrics set to the Caribbean beat of the Atlantic coast. The music, the constant chants, and Borge's speech lambasting the United States and its "lackeys"—the *contras*, or counterrevolutionaries; the opposition group known as the Democratic Coordinator; the anti-Sandinista newspaper *La Prensa*; and the hierarchy of the Catholic Church—are all part of the day's

Map by Brad Wye

entertainment. More sinister forces are at work as well: as the external pressure on Nicaragua has increased, the Sandinistas have increasingly portrayed the remaining opposition voices as traitors linked to the U.S.-backed *contras*.

Several miles away, in another part of Managua, a second outpouring of popular sentiment is under way in the Eastern Market, home since the days of Somoza to a thriving and diverse bazaar. The Sandinistas have tried unsuccessfully to replace this chaotic flea market with cleaner, more modern facilities located throughout the city. Yet Nicaraguans apparently prefer the Eastern Market's endless rows of crowded tables and wooden lean-tos to the concrete, whitewashed, orderly stalls of the official markets. In the days immediately following the "triumph" in 1979, Nicaraguans combed the Eastern Market to buy back possessions looted in the chaos of Somoza's last days. Now, upper-middle-class women send their maids to the market to buy extra toilet paper and toothpaste, and mechanics search for scarce spare parts that Nicaragua can no longer afford to import. With Nicaragua's depleted foreign reserves and the government's emphasis on the poor, a luxury imported item such as wrapping paper costs the same as a mature hen: sixty *córdobas*, or about $2.00 at the official exchange rate. At the illegal black-market rate for the dollar, the same item would cost about ten cents; those with access to dollars can live very well indeed.

The women vendors of the Eastern Market, known for aggressively confronting both Somoza and the Sandinista government's economic policies, are protesting that the Sandinistas' rationing of eight basic foodstuffs such as oil and flour has reduced their profits. Rationing was imposed in 1982 to ensure access for the poor to basic commodities and to give the Sandinistas more direct control over the economy. Economic dislocations caused by Sandinista mismanagement and the *contras*' economic sabotage have caused shortages in basic foodstuffs, medicines, and luxuries. Unless one can afford to pay extra, long lines and shortages are commonplace and are the source of much discontent with the government. The protesting vendors of the Eastern Market are met by the *turbas divinas*, or "divine mobs," as Borge calls them. These are militant Sandinista supporters who turn out in mass to defend government policies and to harass those willing to protest. The *turbas divinas* physically or vocally harassed *La Prensa*, opposition politicans during the 1984 election campaign, and the pope on his 1983 visit.

Four hours northeast of Managua through Nicaragua's broad, rolling countryside, a funeral is being held for health-care workers and teachers killed by CIA-backed counterrevolutionaries. Their crime was working for the Sandinista government in one of the numerous development projects that have gained the Sandinistas support among the populace. From the point of view of the *contras*, anyone working with the Sandinistas in any capacity is a military target. An estimated 4,000 civilians have been killed in the four-year war.

* * *

Nicaragua wasn't always such a polarized nation. Following the triumph of the popular revolution in July 1979, great hopes were shared by all for a new Nicaragua, without the despised Somoza. Although some 90 percent of the population was united in its opposition to Somoza, Nicaraguans were not in agreement on a future economic and political system to replace his. Leaving aside the die-hard reactionaries who never stopped fighting the Sandinistas, there were three competing visions of post-Somoza Nicaragua. The Sandinista leaders, a mix of nationalists and Marxist-Leninists, were determined to restructure Nicaraguan economic and political life to serve the interests of the poor majority. They believed that socialism was the system most appropriate to achieving this goal. But, given Nicaragua's backward state, a private sector, carefully controlled, would be needed in a "mixed" economy—part private, part socialized. Internationally, Nicaragua would be "anti-imperialist" (read, anti-United States) and "nonaligned" (read, no direct link with the Soviet Union), but with strong ties to socialist countries. A second group, while sympathetic to the Sandinistas' goal of helping the poor, placed priority on political change and wanted to establish something that had never existed before in Nicaragua: a democratic system like that in neighboring Costa Rica, with a strong private sector and a friendly attitude toward the United States. A third group, part of the traditional ruling class, was less concerned about economic justice or political freedom and wanted to overthrow Somoza to gain a larger piece of the political and economic pie for themselves. This group looked to a close alliance with the United States.

The Sandinista National Liberation Front (FSLN) began armed opposition to Somoza in 1959. For more than a decade the FSLN had only limited success in hit-and-run attacks. A natural disaster turned events in its favor. After an earthquake devastated Managua in 1972, leaving 10,000 dead, Somoza channeled international humanitarian aid into his own pockets. The upper and professional classes, who had shared in Somoza's economic development of the 1950s and 1960s, felt that corruption and political favoritism had finally reached intolerable levels and began to turn against Somoza. The catalytic event was the January 1978 murder by Somoza's henchmen of one of Nicaragua's most prominent citizens, Pedro Joaquín Chamorro Cardenal, editor of the opposition newspaper, *La Prensa*. Chamorro had led many failed rebellions against Somoza and represented the most respected and viable alternative to the Sandinistas. Some 30,000 Nicaraguans turned out for Chamorro's funeral, and professionals, businessmen, and unions began a series of strikes demanding Somoza's fall. Despite overwhelming opposition, the dictator held on to the last, issuing orders from his bunker to the hated National Guard to bomb cities sympathetic to the Sandinistas. But bombing alone could not stop a nation seemingly united to overthrow him. With the Sandinistas at the gates of Managua, Somoza took U.S. advice and fled. The revolution left 40,000 to 50,000 dead, 100,000 wounded, 40,000 orphans, and an estimated $1.3 billion in war damages. Enormous foreign loans had been contracted and the treasury looted to support Somoza's golden exile in Miami.

The first postrevolutionary government was a five-member junta that included two non-Sandinistas. But the Sandinistas called the shots, as those with the guns in a revolution inevitably do, through a directorate composed of the nine Sandinista *comandantes*, and presented their decisions to the junta. Relations between the increasingly arrogant and doctrinaire Sandinistas and the democratic and nondemocratic opposition quickly went from lukewarm to sour in the summer of 1980. The legislative body, the Council of State, was reduced to a consultative body in May and was stacked with appointed members from the abundant Sandinista mass organizations. Most non-Sandinistas resigned in protest. Censorship of any news remotely connected to the economy or the *contra* war began in August 1980. The two non-Sandinista members of the junta resigned in April 1980, and were replaced with two other non-Sandinistas, including future opposition leader Arturo Cruz. In August 1980, the Sandinistas announced that, contrary to expectations outside Nicaragua, elections would not be held until 1985, and campaigning would not be allowed until 1984.

As Nicaraguans divided among themselves over the future direction of Nicaragua, U.S.-Sandinista relations, never easy, grew increasingly contentious. The legacy of U.S. involvement in Nicaragua gave the Sandinistas ample reason not to trust the "Colossus of the North." The United States had invaded and occupied Nicaragua in the 1920s and 1930s and had handpicked Somoza to head the despised National Guard. From the point of view of the Sandinistas, the United States had stood by its loyal but brutal ally as he ordered the National Guard to defeat the Sandinistas at any cost. The Carter administration wavered, but did not try to remove Somoza until the Sandinistas were practically at the doors of the dictator's bunker. When the United States finally decided that Somoza was a liability, it tried, unsuccessfully, to mediate the removal of Somoza in order to prevent the Sandinistas from coming to power. When no other Latin American state would join its mediation efforts in the Organization of American States (OAS), the United States settled for a series of vague promises from the Sandinistas about respect for human rights, democracy, and a mixed economy.

Once the Sandinistas assumed power, the Carter administration made conciliatory overtures, designed to moderate the revolution, by sending $8 million in disaster relief, supporting Nicaragua's loan requests from multilateral financial institutions, and requesting $75 million in economic assistance from Congress. The Sandinistas were not impressed with the administration's efforts. Congress held up the economic request until June 1980, and the bulk went to nongovernmental, private enterprises and Catholic Church organizations.

For its part, the United States was impatient with the Sandinistas' postponement of elections, the growing Cuban and Eastern bloc presence, and the militarization of Nicaragua. In the last days of his administration, Carter charged the Sandinistas with arming the Salvadoran guerrillas, and suspended the aid package and blocked international financial loans. Despite evidence that aid to the Salvadoran guerrillas had decreased in response to this suspension under the Carter administration, the new Reagan administration canceled the assistance in April 1981. In November 1981, the United States Congress authorized the CIA to assist covertly counterrevolutionary groups already operating against the Sandinistas. The congressional authorization was ostensibly to assist the *contras* to deter Sandinista support for the guerrillas in El Salvador. The *contras* themselves stated from the beginning that their goal was to overthrow the Sandinistas.

In June 1983, after authorizing some $80 million in aid to the *contras* over the previous two years, Congress cut funding for the covert activity. Nevertheless, the *contras*, some 500 strong in 1981, had grown to 15,000 by 1985 and had broadened their political and military base. Not able to occupy any Nicaraguan territory, the *contras* continued to operate out of bases in Honduras and Costa Rica. They caused great loss of life (and were charged with the deaths of innocent civilians), disrupted important economic activities such as the coffee harvest, and required the Sandinistas to institute an unpopular draft and to increase the proportion of the government budget going to military spending beyond the already high levels of the early 1980s—40 to 50 percent by 1985.

Despite the existence of both political and armed opposition, the Sandinistas have many supporters. The country's poor majority have benefited from a government designed to serve their interests and are the prime supporters of the revolution. The Sandinistas, with the aid of some 2,000 Cuban advisers, initiated a successful literacy campaign and dramatically improved rural health care during the early years of the revolution. Those under the age of sixteen—nearly half the population—are among the most ardent supporters of the Sandinistas, though the military draft has created protest and "draft dodgers" among some.

In 1984, presidential and legislative elections were held with limited participation by opposition groups. After several months of haggling with the Sandinistas over campaign conditions, a key opposition coalition, the Democratic Coordinator, chose not to field its presidential candidate, Arturo Cruz. They complained that government censorship of the press and radio and the long-standing prohibition on campaigning and holding public rallies for nongovernment groups, although reduced or suspended in the period immediately preceding the vote, did not permit fair elections. The Sandinista candidate for president,

Daniel Ortega, won 68 percent of the vote. Some parties critical of the Sandinistas from the right and the left did participate and received some 30 percent of the ballots and representation in the legislature. The Sandinistas undermined the credibility of the elections for many of those sympathetic to the revolution when some *comandantes* described the elections as a "bourgeois formality" for foreign consumption, which could not determine who held power, and argued that the Sandinista victory in the revolution gave the FSLN all the legitimacy it needed.

In 1985, U.S.-Nicaraguan relations became both more tense and more confused. Despite massive lobbying by the administration, Congress at first rejected continued aid to the *contras*, though some members successfully encouraged the President to use his emergency powers to declare an economic embargo against Nicaragua. When the Sandinistas gave continued signs of pursuing closer relations with one of their remaining allies, the Soviet Union, many in Congress who had opposed direct military aid to the *contras* voted for $27 million in aid for "humanitarian" purposes. The U.S. aid for food, clothing, and medical supplies kept the rebels in business by allowing them to channel funds raised privately to the purchase of weapons without direct U.S. involvement. Internally, the Sandinistas prepared to move forcefully against the *contras* by evacuating tens of thousands from border areas to create Sandinista "free-fire zones." Border incidents with Honduras and Costa Rica increased, and the possibility that the *contra* war would escalate in ferocity and territory grew. Speculation that the United States was seeking a pretext for direct military involvement, officially denied in Washington, abounded in Nicaragua. A drive to defeat the *contras* within a year served the Sandinistas as justification for the suspension of civil liberties in October of 1985.

Nicaragua is rich in arable land—although only 8 percent of the available land is being used—and is relatively underpopulated. Nine-tenths of the population live on the western slope of the country (where Spanish and *mestizo* heritages dominate); the rest of the population (English-speaking descendants of Jamaican slaves brought to cultivate bananas in the 1800s and descendants of the indigenous Misquito Indians) lives on the Atlantic coast. Agriculture makes up 24 percent of the gross domestic product and accounts for 48 percent of the economically active population. Nicaragua exports cotton, coffee, sugar, beef, seafood, and bananas. The economy remains mixed, with 60 percent of production in private hands and 40 percent in state hands. (Much of the state property consists of the Somoza dynasty's vast enterprises and land—some 20 percent of the land under cultivation—which were expropriated by the Sandinistas and turned into state or cooperative ventures.) Following the revolution, foreign economic assistance and development specialists from Western Europe and the Eastern bloc flowed into Nicaragua to try to offset economic problems caused by the war against Somoza. Except for U.S. aid to El Salvador, Nicaragua currently receives more assistance from countries in the West than any other Central American country.

Key Facts About Nicaragua:

Population: 2,540,000: 61% urban; 39% rural

Area: 130,000 square miles, or about the size of North Carolina

Infant Mortality: 93.7 deaths per 1,000 births

Life Expectancy: 57.6 years

Literacy: 88%

Per Capita Income: US $920

Income Distribution: 3.1 percent of the national income goes to the bottom 20 percent of the population; 42.2 percent of the national income goes to the top 5 percent

Sectoral Composition of Labor Force: 63% agriculture, 20% industry, 17% services

Size of Armed Forces: 50,000 regular; 50,000 trained militia

EL SALVADOR: SOMETIMES THE SEMBLANCE OF NORMALITY

El Salvador's international airport is the largest and most modern in all of Central America. Located some fifty kilometers from the capital, it sits surrounded by the green patchwork of divided and subdivided plots of land that seem to occupy every square inch of the country's overpopulated territory. Constructed in the 1970s, the airport was placed so far from the capital to encourage tourism, for which high-rise hotels had been constructed on the nearby Pacific beaches. But instead of a tourist boom, the late 1970s brought social disintegration and civil war to El Salvador. The high-rise hotels are now mostly deserted and

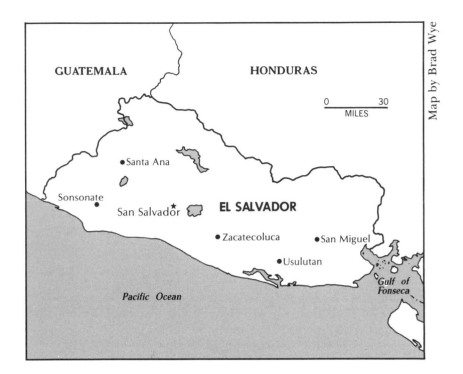

some, in guerrilla-controlled territory, are completely shut down. The modern airport, connected to San Salvador by the country's only four-lane superhighway, serves as a convenience for the North Americans who come to help fight—or report on—the war, not to visit the beaches.

El Salvador is the smallest and most densely populated country in the region. There are 157.3 persons to the square mile, a greater popula-tion density than in India. Overpopulation, coupled with a lack of land and resources, contributed to a war with Honduras in 1969, the migra-tion of several hundred thousand peasants to the capital or to other countries, and the political-economic disaster of the late 1970s and early 1980s. The population has been traditionally concentrated in central and western El Salvador, where the rich volcanic earth produces two of the country's principal exports, coffee and cotton. The relatively underpopulated eastern provinces, hotly disputed by the government and the guerrillas, are now inhabited by only 10 percent of the population.

Before the war El Salvador was the most integrated and in-dustrialized country in Central America, boasting light industry and an extensive structure of paved highways and railroads. Now, any trip begins with inquiries about which roads have been blown up by, or are under the control of, the guerrillas. Until 1985, one could pass within an hour of the capital from government-controlled territory to the "no man's land" of a disputed area to a guerrilla checkpoint where "*los muchachos*" (the boys) collected revolutionary "taxes"—on a strictly "voluntary" basis, of course.

Along the roadside are the *campesinos* (peasants) who live miserable lives in the best of times. Until recently, 2 percent of the population owned 60 percent of the land. Although nationalization of 22 percent of the land under a new reform law has somewhat reduced the concentration of land in the hands of the few, severe land shortages and sharecropping conditions prevail. Many *campesinos* are migrant workers, who follow the harvests in order to earn subsistence wages. For the *campesinos* who live on new cooperatives created by the agrarian reform program, life is better. But lack of credits and of technical assistance still threatens the viability of areas affected by the reform.

Human development did not accompany El Salvador's considerable industralization in the 1960s and 1970s: per-capita income is among the lowest in the region. The majority of the country does not have access to safe drinking water. Mothers have no choice but to give their babies foul water that may well cause diarrhea and dehydration and add another statistic to El Salvador's infant mortality rate. Access to health care is available through church relief workers and doctors who risk their lives by caring for the poor. Those who help the poor are considered to be "subversive" by the army and the right and have been frequent targets of the death squads.

Access to primary education, always minimal outside the cities, has deteriorated since the war began; teachers don't want to go where bullets fly. Half the population is illiterate. Nevertheless, there are more radio stations and a higher newspaper readership in El Salvador than in any other Central American country.

In El Salvador, it is almost impossible to find anyone, regardless of his or her background, who has not lost a loved one to one side or the other since 1979. Even the wealthy are not immune to killings and kidnappings by the guerrillas. But the poor have been hit the hardest by the war. Poor people are trapped in the middle, and most families have suffered abuses from both sides, often repeatedly. Both the guerrillas and the army suspect those who hesitate to demonstrate their loyalty. Although political deaths have greatly decreased (5,331 in 1982; 1,677 in 1983; some 800 in 1984; 250 in the first nine months of 1985) and limited democracy has come, it is still not safe to express a preference for the left. Trying to determine which side a *campesino* is on is almost impossible. Allegiances can change quickly, depending on whether the guerrillas or the army is in town. Particularly desperate are the more then 500,000 displaced Salvadorans who live in makeshift camps and are continually suspect as guerrilla sympathizers.

The guerrillas number 5,000 to 7,000 and are supported logistically by *las masas* (the masses). The *masas* are civilians (largely peasants) who provide the guerrillas with food, clothing, and shelter, and serve as messengers, sources of information, and other support necessary to their operations. U.S. government counterinsurgency experts estimate that for every guerrilla there are approximately ten *masas*, or roughly 1 percent of the population, who are active supporters of the guerrillas.

The Salvadoran guerrillas are composed of a military side, the Farabundo Martí Liberation Front (FMLN) and a political side, the Democratic Revolutionary Front (FDR). The FMLN, consisting of five guerrilla groups, takes its name from 1930s communist peasant leader Farabundo Martí, who died in the bloody *matanza* (massacre) of 1932. The FDR-FMLN represents a variety of political ideologies, from center-left democrats to a majority of Marxist-Leninists, with different views about the best road to power.

The conditions to produce a social upheaval in El Salvador had existed for decades: poverty among the masses, extreme wealth for a tiny oligarchy, brutal repression, and corrupt politics. The spark to light the fuse of revolution proved to be the rapid economic growth that came to El Salvador in the 1960s and 1970s. The country's tiny middle class was strengthened and expanded by the economic activity, but found it had no political representation. The traditional oligarchy tried to maintain its hold on political power by enlisting the military to protect its interests. Nineteen hundred seventy-two proved to be a fateful year. José Napoléon Duarte, the reformist Christian Democratic mayor of San Salvador, stood for president with a running mate, Guillermo Ungo, who represented a block of left, socialist, and communist parties. Duarte and Ungo won the election but lost the count when the military suspended the election returns running in Duarte's favor and announced their own candidate as the winner. After leading an abortive coup against the military's theft of the election, Duarte was imprisoned, tortured, and exiled. The United States, which would later regret a missed opportunity, did nothing to support this peaceful attempt at reform by Duarte and Ungo.

Given the failure of the ballot to achieve change, "popular organizations" of peasants, workers, students, church sectors, and some elements of the middle class adopted nontraditional means of protest. Their land seizures, strikes, and peaceful factory and foreign embassy sit-ins were met with violent repression.

The Salvadoran civil war began in earnest after the October 1979 coup led by reformist military officers against the military dictator, Carlos Humberto Romero. Younger officers had been shocked by the overthrow of Somoza in nearby Nicaragua and feared that, unless basic reforms were instituted, social pressures in El Salvador could lead to a similar explosion and the demise of the armed forces. They followed an old dictum of the Latin American military that when the bulls are stampeding it is safer to lead them onto higher ground than to try to turn them from their course. Better, they thought, to lead a reform than to try to hold back a revolution. Inviting civilians into the junta, the military announced an extensive land-reform program and the nationalization of the country's banks and the coffee-export trade.

Their reformist coup, however, unleashed the pent-up forces of El Salvador's highly polarized society. Some on the left used the political opening to try to push for more drastic changes, others, for a true socialist revolution. The traditional right and more conservative officers sought to reverse the reformist moves of the younger officers and initiated a massive repression employing the infamous *escuadrones de muerte* (death squads)—paramilitary gangs linked to the military and orchestrated by the oligarchy—that turned El Salvador into a slaughterhouse. Each morning in San Salvador found new piles of brutally murdered and mutilated bodies on street corners, garbage dumps, and at the bottom of ravines.

Among the dead were many of the leaders of El Salvador's "popular organizations." This program of political assassination radicalized some leaders who had often been considered moderate in the Salvadoran context. Guillermo Ungo, Duarte's former running mate in 1972, left the reformist junta, eventually to become the chief spokesperson for the guerrillas' political arm, the FDR. Rubén Zamora, at one time a member of Duarte's party and a cabinet member of the reformist junta, abandoned democratic politics when his brother, Mario, the country's attorney general, was assassinated in his home while Rubén slept next door. He would join Ungo in representing the FDR-FMLN internationally.

Although many of the reformist junta's early supporters went into opposition when they felt the junta had been fatally compromised by repression and the resurgence of right-wing officers, Duarte and the United States did not. Fearing a complete victory by the left, the United States rushed assistance to the Salvadoran military and attempted to shore up a government on the point of collapse. Total U.S. aid to El Salvador had been $16.8 million from 1946 to 1979. In 1980 and early 1981 the Carter administration delivered $10.7 million in "nonlethal" and lethal military aid plus a substantial economic-assistance package.

The salvage operation worked after a fashion. A "general offensive" by the guerrillas, modeled after the Sandinista victory in Nicaragua and designed to present President Reagan with a fait accompli on his inauguration, failed to spark the mass uprising that the guerrillas had expected. Additional military "trainers" from the United States and $25 million in military aid demonstrated in March 1981 that President

Reagan was also committed to backing the civilian-military junta. Duarte, not much more than a figurehead for the military, had his reformist credentials severely tested as he presided over one of the most repressive periods in El Salvador's bloody history in 1980 and 1981.

Constituent Assembly elections in March of 1982 produced a victory for a coalition of right-wing parties led by former major Roberto D'Aubuisson's ARENA party. Only strong pressure from the United States prevented D'Aubuisson from being named as provisional president. D'Aubuisson, who had been cashiered from the army because of his extreme politics, represented a far-right-wing response to El Salvador's civil war. Rumored to be linked directly to the death squads and to the murder of Archbishop Oscar Romero, a liberal church leader, D'Aubuisson was viewed as an unacceptable partner for the United States by much of the U.S. Congress. His party enjoyed popular support, however, in the countryside among landowners, some of the peasantry, and with the urban business sector. Through mid-1985, he would remain a strong brake on attempts at continuing the reforms of the 1979 junta.

With support from the United States and reported CIA funding, Duarte was elected president of El Salvador for the second time in 1984 and, this time, allowed to take office. Hamstrung by a Legislative Assembly dominated by the right wing, Duarte struggled throughout 1984 to gain the confidence of the armed forces, put the guerrillas on the defensive, and restore his image as a reformist politician. Amid grave economic reversals and predictions of defeat for his Christian Democratic party, Duarte emerged the surprising victor from new legislative and municipal elections in 1985, perhaps because of his equally unexpected, and so far unproductive, opening to the guerrillas in late 1984. D'Aubuisson and the traditional right received a crushing defeat at the polls and entered into a period of reexamination that led to D'Aubuisson's removal as leader of ARENA. Attacked by the wounded right as having stolen the election for the Christian Democrats, the military found itself in the pleasant but historically unprecedented position of defender of the democratic process. Whether the military has forsaken its bloody past for the way of democracy or merely made a marriage of convenience with the political arrangement most likely to guarantee its continued influence is a key question for the country's future.

In 1985, El Salvador was more stable politically than it had been for years. Its popular president seemed to be fulfilling his vision of himself as the savior of his country. The U.S. Congress continued to be pleased by the progress made politically and militarily and willing to maintain funding that had become crucial to El Salvador's daily survival. (Since

1981, U.S. military and economic assistance to El Salvador has totaled $1.4 billion, or $280 for every man, woman, and child in the country.) The war with the guerrillas remained stalemated, the economy in shambles, and political stability balanced too directly on the person of Napoleón Duarte. But the United States' position in El Salvador was stronger than at any time since 1979.

By mid-1985 there were signs that a politically and militarily weaker guerrilla movement was changing strategy. Political assassinations and kidnappings, targeted on North Americans as well as Salvadorans, increased, and the mobilization of workers and other "popular forces" that had been so prominent in 1979-80 reappeared. The air war against the guerrillas became a key element of the counterinsurgency strategy, while opponents of the policy raised concerns about possible civilian casualties and forced evacuations. The optimism in Washington seemed belied by the conclusions of Salvadorans from different parts of the political spectrum that the economy could not tolerate another year of war without collapse.

Key Facts About El Salvador:

Population: 4.9 million: 41% urban 59% rural

Area: 21,000 square miles, or about the size of Massachusetts

Infant Mortality: 42.6 deaths per 1000 births

Life Expectancy: 62 years

Literacy: 62%

Per Capita Income: US $1130

Income Distribution: 5.8 percent of the national income goes to the bottom 20 percent of the population; 21.4 percent of the national income goes to the top 5 percent

Sectoral Composition of Labor Force: 55% agriculture; 21% industry; 24% services

Size of Armed Forces: 40,000

HONDURAS: WANTED—A BETTER DEAL

Tegucigalpa's Central Park was filled to capacity for the political rally. Beginning at the heavily guarded, somewhat baroque presidential palace, the line of march to protest recent tax increases had moved through the winding, narrow streets of the capital's downtown to the central square. Thousands of workers, students, and party faithful were assembled to hear the government of President Suazo Córdova attacked for the cruel economic burden it was imposing on the workers of Honduras with its new tax program. Never popular in any society, these taxes seemed particularly irksome because they came at a time of severe economic recession in Honduras and because they would not go to fund education, health, or welfare programs. Instead they would be used to fuel the dramatic increases in military spending required by the United States' use of Honduras as a strategic staging area and military exercise site.

As the afternoon wore on the speeches from the podium gradually changed. The focus on taxes, jobs, corruption, and the person of the president shifted, and the United States was heard, at first infrequently and then more often, as the object of attack. Only a few weeks before, a

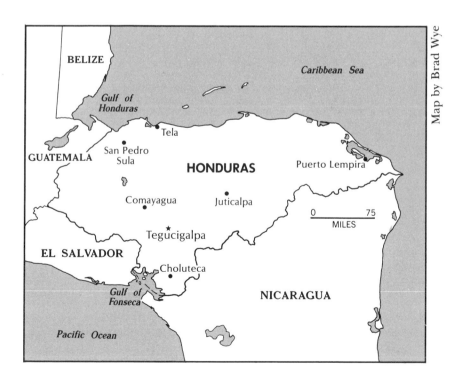

traffic accident involving U.S. military personnel had become a nasty incident as university students overturned and set fire to the car. Honduran and U.S. officials alike stressed that the car burning was an aberration in the typically warm state of U.S.-Honduran relations.

* * *

At the U.S. Embassy perched on the side of a hill overlooking the lush mountains surrounding Tegucigalpa, the philosophical debate between the military officer and the North American visitor over the effectiveness of the *contras* as an instrument of U.S. pressure against Nicaragua took a practical turn:

> "I don't know if the *contras* can overthrow the Sandinistas or not. But I'll tell you one thing: if we don't continue funding them, they'll sure as hell overthrow this government."

* * *

It is ironic that once-sleepy Honduras, the original "banana republic," should be at the center of the Central American conflict. The butt of jokes, its capital referred to as Teguci*golpe* because of the frequency of *golpes de estado*, or coups against the government, Honduras is now crucial to the support of U.S. policy in both El Salvador and Nicaragua. It will be the site from which direct U.S. military involvement in the region will be launched if it is ever to be used.

Yet Honduras is a fragile base upon which to build such weighty policies. In 1981, the country held its first direct elections for president and congress in over twenty-five years. Ending a decade of direct military rule, the elections may in retrospect mark the beginning of a transition to true civilian control, or they may represent a return to a civilian puppet government for the military that has been the customary form of Honduran politics for a generation. In November 1985, national elections for president and the legislature provided the first democratic transition from one civilian president to another in fifty years.

Like the rest of Central America, except Costa Rica, Honduras has been struggling to accommodate new political actors into a game dominated by traditional elites relying on the military to defend their privileges. But for unique historical reasons, the poor and disadvantaged in Honduras have been less strident in their demands on the system and the military more disposed to adopt modest reform to try to preempt social pressure before it became explosive. Honduras is also the last Central American country to retain working remnants of the nineteenth-century Liberal and Conservative (in Honduras, Nationalist) parties. Factionalized and elitist, the parties have, nevertheless, served to articulate public opinion and motivate voter participation. In the elections of 1981, a turnout of over 80 percent of registered voters cast over 90 percent of the ballots for either the Nationalists or the Liberals. Dr. Roberto Suazo Cordova, a physician from Honduras' second city of San Pedro Sula, led the temporarily united factions of the Liberal party to a 52 to 40 percent defeat of the Nationalists. In 1985, confusing electoral procedures gave the presidency to Liberal candidate José Azcona Hoyo, even though he had received fewer votes than the leading Nationalist candidate, Rafael Leonardo Callejas.

Analysts have viewed the victory of the Liberals over the Nationalists (traditionally backed by the military) in 1981 and 1985 as indicating popular skepticism about the value of the military's influence on politics. Yet since 1981 the military has repeatedly preserved its political prerogatives through the mechanism of its powerful policy-making group, the Supreme Council of the Armed Forces (CONSUFFAA). In the fall of 1983, then-Commander-in-Chief General Gustavo Alvarez Martínez, signed an agreement with the United States to establish a Regional Military Training Center (CREM) for Hondurans and Salvadorans, then surrounded the capital with troops and announced the decision to the legislature and president. In March 1984, President Suazo and some junior officers pulled a surprise reverse coup on Alvarez and ousted him, apparently because of his disregard for customary collegial decision making in the armed forces and his close identification with U.S. interests in Honduras. The new commander-in-chief, General Walter López, while operating in more traditional style for a Honduran commander and serving notice that the United States will have to compensate Honduras more generously for its support of U.S. strategic interests in the region, has also made unilateral decisions about national policy and informed the president after the fact.

The key issue of U.S.-Honduran relations, for civilian and military circles alike, is Honduras' current role as the center of U.S. military operations in the region. Since 1980, Honduras has allowed anti-Sandinista forces (the *contras*), at present totaling some 12,000 and growing, to operate out of its territory. Hondurans fear that a permanent cut in U.S. Congressional aid for the *contras* could leave a very destablizing group of 12,000-plus armed guerrillas inside the country. As the fortunes of the *contras* have risen and fallen with the U.S. Congress, the Honduran military has moved to restrict or expand the freedom of the *contras* to operate inside Honduras.

The United States Regional Military Training Center, established in 1983, had been used to train Salvadoran and a much smaller number of Honduran troops in Honduras. The center could train Salvadorans at lower costs than would be entailed in transporting them to a U.S. facility, and it avoided the politically difficult alternative of raising the number of U.S. military trainers inside El Salvador, set at fifty-five by an understanding between Congress and the Executive Branch. Yet Honduras always considered El Salvador its primary regional adversary. El Salvador invaded Honduras in the 1969 "Soccer War," and the two countries have an unreconciled border dispute. In 1984, General López unilaterally suspended the use of the Training Center for Salvadorans, eventually closed it completely, and announced the need for a new security treaty between the United States and Honduras.

The United States has established a large military presence and substantial infrastructure in Honduras. U.S.-Honduran joint military exercises have occurred virtually nonstop since August 1983, involving up to 5,000 U.S. troops at a time and costing the United States at least $100 million. In addition, there are an undisclosed number of U.S. military officers flying intelligence reconnaissance missions over El Salvador and Nicaragua and assisting the *contras* in their war against the Sandinistas. The U.S. military's construction over the past two years has included hospitals, airports, listening stations, trenches, living quarters, etc. The U.S. government denies that any of these facilities are permanent or intended for possible use in a direct U.S. invasion of Nicaragua. However, should the United States decide to undertake direct military action, all the logistical preparations are in place in Honduras.

Some analysts argue that there is growing resentment of the United States for its use of Honduras as a proxy. In late 1984, Honduras formally requested a better deal. Militarily, Honduras asked for revisions in the 1954 bilateral military assistance agreement to clarify the growing U.S. presence in Honduras, a separate bilateral security arrangement, and more training of Hondurans in the Regional Training Center. Four hundred million dollars in assistance over the next several years was requested to bolster the Honduran economy, which faces low prices for bananas and coffee, the region's lowest per capita income ($600), negative economic growth rates since 1982, and heavy expenditures for its contribution to the joint military exercises.

In fiscal year 1984, the United States gave Honduras $77.5 million in military aid and $152 million in economic aid. In fiscal year 1985, Honduras will receive about $63 million in military aid and about $116.5 million in economic aid.

Hondurans are not united in their outlook on close U.S.-Honduran security ties. Generally speaking, Honduras harbors less animosity toward the United States than do Guatemala, El Salvador, or Nicaragua, despite the pervasiveness of North American culture and economy in the country since United Fruit first set up its headquarters there in 1909. Many feel that acting as the U.S. proxy can lead only to trouble; others argue that it is the best protection against the Sandinistas. Still others worry that the military emphasis of policy in the area strengthens the hand of the armed forces to the detriment of civilians in government, Honduras' uniquely vibrant trade unions, and its relatively free press. In 1985, there was evidence that the Honduran military, traditionally less repressive than those of its neighbors, was beginning to commit the same human rights abuses common elsewhere in the region. Refugee camps were attacked by Honduran soldiers looking for Salvadoran guerrillas, and a former officer and critic of close U.S.-Honduran ties was found brutally murdered. U.S. support for the contras also received a jolt when Honduras, in the heat of the November elections, prevented overt, "humanitarian" aid from being transferred to the Nicaraguan resistance on Honduran territory.

Key Facts About Honduras:

Population: 3,942,000: 38% urban; 62% rural

Area: 112,000 square miles, or about the size of Louisiana

Infant Mortality: 87 deaths per 1000 births

Life Expectancy: 60 years

Literacy: 59.5%

Per Capita Income: US $600

Income Distribution: 3.0 percent of the national income goes to the bottom 20 percent of the population; 29.0 percent of the national income goes to the top 5 percent

Sectoral Composition of Labor Force: 63% agriculture; 20% industry; 17% services

Size of Armed Forces: 15,200

COSTA RICA:
"OUR WEAKNESS IS OUR DEFENSE"

The road to the town of Liberia is a pleasant one that winds its way through Costa Rica's lush central highlands, then drops down to the flat plains of this country's "Wild West." A trip through the verdant countryside tells one a great deal about Costa Rica. Modest homes of wood and cement dot the landscape. There is poverty to be sure, but little of the squalor that dominates much of rural Latin America. Schools appear at roadsides in population centers of any size and

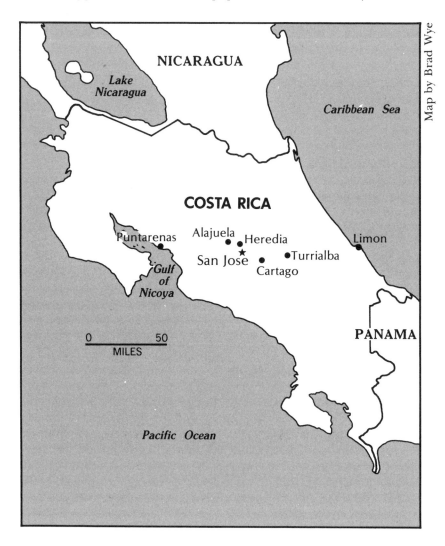

Map by Brad Wye

brilliant white clinics with neat red crosses are visible from time to time. The metaphor for what makes Costa Rica different from the rest of Central America may well be the passing lanes of the country's major highways. Driving an automobile in Latin America is usually intimately connected with asserting one's manhood; risks are taken routinely to demonstrate that death can be challenged and beaten. How "un-Latin," then, of the Costa Ricans to provide safe passing on hills. Absent is the joy of pulling out from behind a belching bus to encounter another driver closing in at breakneck speed from the opposite direction. In Costa Rica, one is reduced to motoring calmly around the offending vehicle at the next appropriate passing zone.

Costa Rican politics has for decades provided a passing lane for political passions. Since 1948, free and open elections have offered a highly literate population a voice in national life. In that same year, a generation's worth of progressive social legislation was ratified, a standing army abolished, and a civic culture favoring compromise and the peaceful settlement of disputes instituted. In Central America, Costa Rica is not merely unique, it is virtually miraculous.

The drive to Liberia inevitably raises the question of whether Costa Rica can remain an island of peace in a region at war. A few kilometers outside the town lies the third-rate airport of Llano Grande. Here in the late 1970s, at the only suitable site close to the Nicaraguan border, the Sandinistas flew in supplies for their war against Somoza. In the mid-1980s, the United States proposed to expand the runway to accommodate jet planes—ostensibly to bring in tourists for the nearby beaches. If the site was also an excellent base for raids on Managua by anti-Sandinista rebels or for surveillance aircraft, that was just so much coincidence.

Whatever Washington's intentions in making its offer, the Costa Rican government decided to decline it. But there are still other offers, most recently one by the U.S. Information Agency to a private Costa Rican broadcasting station to set up a powerful radio transmitter on the Nicaraguan border. Whether it will become the equivalent of Radio Free Nicaragua or merely convey the Costa Rican brand of *salsa* music to the Nicaraguans is unclear. José Figueres, the hero of 1948, says the government must nationalize the station should it become a propaganda weapon against the Nicaraguans. President Luis Alberto Monge, trying to tread a fine line between the left and the right in his country, inaugurated the new facility, denying it will violate his 1983 proclamation of Costa Rica's neutrality. Perhaps Costa Rica will once again decline to enter the thicket of Central American politics. But those same Sandinistas who operated out of Llano Grande six years ago have denounced the station as part of the "imperialist U.S. plot" against Nicaragua.

Back in Costa Rica's capital of San José, a Honduran and a North American visitor watch as President Monge and other politicians address a mildly enthusiastic crowd of schoolchildren who have been given the day off to celebrate Costa Rica's proclamation of neutrality. The speeches, although florid in the Latin style, are amazingly short. The entire rally lasts little more than an hour. As President Monge slowly descends from the podium, a boy and girl stand at his side guiding his steps. The president then walks among the crowd, virtually without security. The Honduran wonders aloud when his country will be able to achieve the political maturity of these Costa Ricans. The North American ponders his country's policies. Are they helping to preserve this precious outpost of democracy or, in the interest of broader regional objectives, do they risk sacrificing it to the chaos that consumes so much of Central America?

* * *

Costa Rica's contemporary political arrangements stem directly from the "revolution" of 1948. In the "revolution," a collection of anticommunist forces from different parts of the political spectrum combined to overthrow a coalition government of moderate conservatives, progressive forces in the Catholic Church, and a strong communist party—a coalition that could only make sense in Latin America. Progressive social policies such as social security legislation and a strong income-tax law and the increasing influence of communists in the government sparked opposition. But the immediate impetus for the revolt was the rigging of the elections of 1948 to maintain the government coalition in power. Protests over the election results mushroomed into armed conflict led by a successful landowner, José ("Pepe") Figueres Ferrer. His forces of National Liberation, with assistance from a United States worried about communist influence, defeated the standing army of the government and ushered in a new era of Costa Rican politics.

In victory, National Liberation set precedents of civility and compromise that would mark Costa Rican politics down to the present day. It abolished many unions and outlawed the communist party that had been particularly strong among organized banana workers. But it also instituted a major tax on wealth, eliminated a standing army, and extended full political rights to women and blacks. After ruling for an interim period, Figueres returned political power to the true victor of the 1948 election and formed his own political party, the National Liberation party (PLN), which adopted many of the progressive reforms of the prior coalition government as its own platform. Although elected to the presidency in 1953 (with "Don Pepe" as its candidate), the PLN has frequently turned over power to the opposition in electoral contests that have been largely free and fair. Under PLN leadership, the government's role in the economy grew through the nationalization of the country's bank, insurance, transportation, and utility industries, and the joint public-private financing of many productive enterprises. Other legislation enacted social welfare programs for medical care, social security, housing subsidies, and numerous other services to benefit the middle class and, to a lesser extent, the lower class.

The "revolution of 1948" helped Costa Rica avoid many of the political problems that affected the rest of Central America. But it could not eliminate the economic problems that afflicted all of the small Central American exporters in the late 1970s and 1980s. In the worldwide recession of the late 1980s, prices for Costa Rica's main exports—coffee and bananas—fell drastically, while expenditures for imported oil escalated. To cover the gap between earnings and expenditures and to maintain the country's politically popular consumer-goods imports, Costa Rica borrowed heavily on the international market. When international credit dried up in 1981-1982, Costa Rica nearly went bankrupt. Austerity programs, international aid, rescheduled loans, and declining oil prices stabilized the country in the early 1980s, while Costa Rica sought longer-term solutions to its economic crisis.

As economic problems stabilized, due in part to massive U.S. aid ($336 million from 1981 to 1984; $175 million in 1985), political problems multiplied. Real declines in most Costa Ricans' standard of living activated Costa Rica's unions and drove the rural poor into burgeoning squatter settlements around the major cities. Middle-class dissatisfaction with the elimination of government subsidies could no longer be bought off by a government strapped for operating funds.

Foreign-policy problems intruded ever more strongly into the already confused domestic scene. The continued radicalization of the Sandinista revolution polarized Costa Rican politics. In 1984 a Nicaraguan "draft dodger" was alleged to have been forcibly removed by Sandinista police from asylum in the Costa Rican Embassy in Managua. Costa Rican housewives marched on the presidential palace carrying pairs of trousers and demanded that President Luis Alberto Monge "put on his pants" and act tough by breaking diplomatic relations with Nicaragua and invoking the Rio treaty of mutual defense with the United States. In the campaign leading up to the February 1986 presidential and congressional elections, massive funding from the U.S. Republican party was alleged to be flowing to the National Liberation party's opposition, which promised to move Costa Rica more closely to the U.S. position in Central America. Meanwhile, thousands of Costa Ricans were reported to be fighting *with* the Sandinistas *against* the *contras*, and Monge's government accepted U.S. Special Forces advisers to train elements of Costa Rica's National Guard in counterinsurgency in case these Costa Rican supporters of the Sandinistas decided to practice their martial arts at home in the future. Border conflicts increased as *contra* operations out of Costa Rica, denied officially by the government, grew. The death of two Costa Rican border guards in 1985 threatened to permanently rupture Costa Rican-Nicaraguan relations.

Key Facts About Costa Rica:

Population: 2,330,000: 83% urban; 16% rural

Area: 51,000 square miles, or about the size of Arkansas

Infant Mortality: 17.9 deaths per 1,000 births

Life Expectancy: 74 years

Literacy: 90%

Per Capita Income: US $1430

Income Distribution: 3.3 percent of the national income goes to the bottom 20 percent of the population; 39.5 percent of the national income goes to the top 5 percent

Sectoral Composition of Labor Force: 29% agricultural; 23% industry; 48% services

Size of Armed Forces: 7,000 Rural and Civil Guard

GUATEMALA: WAR WITHOUT END

Nearly 5,000 Guatemalans have been seized without warrant and killed since General Lucas García became president of Guatemala in 1978. The bodies of the victims have been found piled up in ravines, dumped at roadsides or buried in mass graves. Thousands bore the scars of torture, and death had come to most by strangling with a garrotte, by being suffocated in rubber hoods or by being shot in the head.
—Amnesty International, *Guatemala: A Government Program of Political Murder* (London), February 1981.

A dramatic instance which seems to substantiate charges of government cooperation in the activities of the death squads was the attempted assassination of student leader Manuel Valvert at San Carlos [the national university], which was bungled in June 1980. One of the three hit men escaped, but students seized the other two, who turned out to be a member of the *Policía de Hacienda* [Treasury police] and a member of the S-2 intelligence section of the army. The S-2 man was taken to the main gate of the university, doused with gasoline, and publicly burned to death. Valvert, who had been wounded in the attempt on his life and could not have taken part in this burning, was then arrested at his hospital bed, and charged with the crime.... By the end of [1980], eighty-six

Map by Brad Wye

university professors, three hundred eighty-nine students, and a number of other persons at the university had been killed.

* * *

The thirty peasants had herded the [Spanish] embassy personnel and others, including two distinguished Guatemalans, former Vice President Eduardo Caceres Lehnhoff and former Foreign Minister Adolfo Molina Orantes, both of whom happened to be visiting [the embassy], into a small room. As the police came in shooting, one of the peasants dropped the molotov cocktail he had been holding. In the resultant holocaust, thirty-nine persons burned to death, including all but one of the peasants. The one peasant survivor was badly burned and taken to San Juan de Dios Hospital, where he was seized, dragged off, and murdered by a death squad the same day. Both of the distinguished Guatemalans were killed but, unfortunately for the government, the Spanish ambassador himself escaped, by some miracle, and he promptly accused the police of excessive violence. In protest, Spain immediately closed its embassy.
—Thomas P. Anderson, *Politics in Central America* (New York: Praeger, 1983).

* * *

The record of Guatemalan politics since the CIA-engineered coup that overthrew the elected government of Colonel Jacobo Arbenz in 1954 should give pause to those who believe that democratic politics can be installed in Central America by armed force. Since that date, military government has followed military government (with some brief civilian interludes); coups or rigged elections have been the routine means of changing national leaders; and a guerrilla movement founded by young, reformist military officers grew during the 1960s. In 1984, for the first time in thirty years, Guatemala began to show signs of moving toward civilian rule and more open politics. But doubts about the development of real democracy lingered.

The fraudulent election of General Romeo Lucas García in March 1978 ushered in a new period of extreme repression of political liberties and of human-rights abuses. A guerrilla movement supposedly crushed in the 1960s reappeared and threatened for the first time to forge links to Guatemala's majority Indian population. Lucas' ultraconservative military government instituted a "scorched-earth" policy against the guerrillas and the Indians. Those suspected of sympathizing with the guerrillas were massacred, and their villages, crops, and livestock destroyed.Guatemala had lost U.S. economic and military assistance in 1977 when it refused to meet President Jimmy Carter's human rights requirements for aid. With political deaths averaging some 600 a month throughout the late 1970s and early 1980s,

Guatemala became an international pariah. Oblivious to world opinion, Guatemala preferred to fight its insurgency ruthlessly without the external restraints that would accompany foreign aid.

In March 1982, another rigged election brought Lucas García's hand-picked candidate, General Angel Aníbal Guevara, into the presidential office. Charges of fraud by the political parties were rampant, and much of the military opposed continuation of a Lucas García-style government. Seventeen days after the election, six junior military officers led a bloodless coup to prevent Guevara's inauguration. They called upon retired General Efraín Ríos Montt—their former instructor at the military college—to head a new military government.

Ríos Montt, an evangelical Christian in predominantly Catholic Guatemala, was portrayed initially as a reformer concerned about human rights. However, his government continued the crackdown on political activists, guerrillas, and Indians. A civic-action program to ensure the allegiance of the Indians was developed. Ríos Montt's so-called beans-and-rifles strategy involved organizing Indians into civil-defense patrols in return for access to food and health care and, once again, seemed to beat back the guerrilla threat. But dissatisfaction within the military's ranks prompted a coup against Ríos Montt in August 1983. The high command, under the leadership of General Oscar Humberto Mejía Victores, had reacted to Ríos Montt's managerial incompetence, infusion of religion into political and military matters, and to the international isolation of Guatemala.

General Mejía Victores remained commander-in-chief of the Guatemalan armed forces and the de facto head of state until the elections of November 1985. He governed by decree, after conferring with a group of military advisers. Despite the apparent destruction of the guerrilla forces, the Mejía Victores government remained preoccupied with a possible resumption of the insurgency. Consequently, the government concentrated on denying the guerrillas support by incorporating the Indians into national life through participation in civil-defense forces and resettlement to so-called model villages, and on improving Guatemala's chances to obtain international economic and military assistance. Deaths attributable to human-rights abuses declined to an average of ninety per month in 1985, and some opening of the political system began under his rule.

General Mejía moved to improve the domestic climate and to foster better relations with the United States and with the rest of Latin America by holding elections to a Constituent Assembly in July 1984, the first elections without substantial fraud since 1954. The Constituent Assembly was charged with framing a new constitution and overseeing presidential elections set for November 1985. In return for this political opening, the military hoped to gain diplomatic acceptance for Guatemala among its neighbors and in the United States, as well as the restoration of badly needed economic and military assistance.

In the presidential elections of 1985, a crowded field of candidates ranging ideologically from the center to the extreme right competed in a first round in November. When none obtained an absolute majority, a runoff was held that pitted centrist Christian Democrat Marco Vinicio Cerezo Arévalo against center-right newspaper magnate Jorge Carpio Nicolle. Although accused of being a leftist by Carpio, Cerezo was careful to avoid any mention of land reform in his campaign and to deny that he would investigate the army for political assassinations and disappearances. In the December runoff Cerezo won 68 percent of the vote to 32 percent for his opponent. Vowing to aggressively seek U.S. aid, Cerezo said, "They've owed it to us for a long time."

The Guatemalan military's commitment to democratization remains untested. Some sectors support the restoration of civilian government; others harbor their own political ambitions and, after thirty years of power, are unwilling to allow the civilians an opportunity to govern. The military's respect for the new constitution and for President Cerezo's independence will be the crucial indicators of their commitment to civilian government.

Guatemala's agricultural economy is in a disastrous state because of low prices for its principal exports—coffee, sugar and cotton—a $2.3 billion foreign debt, and 40 percent unemployment and underemployment. Given its poor human-rights record, foreign governments and banks have been unwilling to assist Guatemala's economic recovery or to contribute to the maintenance of its 30,000-man armed forces. The tentative democratization has improved Guatemala's relations within Latin America and has increased Guatemala's chances for renewed assistance from the United States. The U.S. Congress appropriated $300,000 for military training and $29.6 million for economic assistance in 1984. Both economic and military assistance are likely to increase in 1986, as the Reagan administration attempts to gain influence in previously isolated Guatemala now that a civilian president has been installed.

Key Facts About Guatemala:

Population: 7,411,000: 41% urban; 59% rural

Area: 109,000 square miles, or about the size of Kentucky

Infant Mortality: 66.5 deaths per 1,000 births

Life Expectancy: 60 years

Literacy: 47%

Per Capita Income: US $1,130

Income Distribution: 5.0 percent of the national income goes to the bottom 20 percent of the population; 35.0 percent of the national income goes to the top 5 percent

Sectoral Composition of Labor Force: 55% agriculture; 21% industry; 24% services

Size of Armed Forces: 30,000

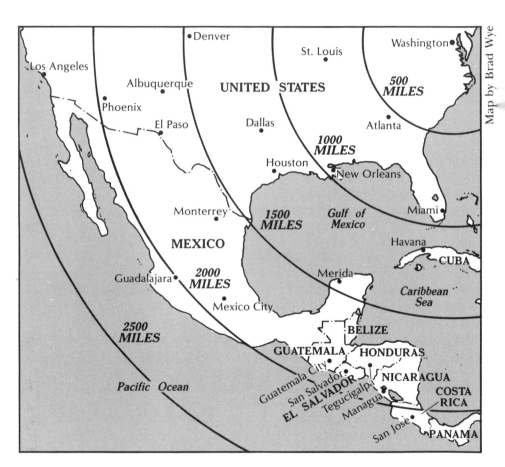

Map by Brad Wye

"San Salvador is closer to Houston, Texas, than Houston is to Washington, D.C."
—President Ronald Reagan, May 1984

3 Five Countries and Ten Questions: The Policy Debate

President John F. Kennedy is said to have remarked about Washington, D.C., that it combined northern charm and southern efficiency: neither attractive nor a good place to get much done. Perhaps he would have modified his harsh words if he had lived to the 1980s, when many American cities were in decline and Washington continued to expand, added one of the most beautiful subway systems in the world, and became much more cosmopolitan.

But it is curious how Washington both attracts and repels its citizens. Since 1976, it has been in vogue for national politicians to run against Washington. According to these politicians, Washington, as the symbol of the federal government, is to be blamed for what is wrong in voters' lives. The home of "big government," Washington regulates, restricts, interferes, requires, legislates, overspends, and, above all, overtaxes a citizenry which, if left to its own devices, could achieve a more harmonious union. Being against Washington and the evil deeds done there is to be on the side of all that has made America great.

Yet many of those who come to Washington to do the nation's business contract "Potomac fever"—a fascination with the power and prestige that emanate from Washington—and never want to leave. Potomac fever affects not only senators, congressmen, presidents, and cabinet officers, but also their staffs and the panoply of policy analysts, "think-tankers," lobbyists, public relations experts, and others who earn their living from, and bask in the reflected glory of, the fact that decisions affecting the nation's and the world's future are made "inside the Beltway."

To understand policy debates in Washington, it is helpful to know something about what shapes the attitudes and behavior of those who make policy and those who make it their business to develop an alternative, "better" policy than the one being followed. Stereotypical portraits of two types of people who make and unmake policy in Washington are presented below. The "national security analyst" and the "human rights activist" rarely exist in the form in which they are presented here and do not exhaust the range of policy "types." But they are especially relevant for a discussion of U.S. policy toward Central America.

There are many ways in which North Americans are divided over Central America. The division between those concerned primarily about the protection of U.S. interests in the world and strategic threats to those interests from Central America and those focused on the promotion and protection of Central Americans' human rights is among the most basic. Our purpose in stereotyping a fictitious "national security analyst" and a "human rights activist" is not to criticize either, but to illustrate the ways in which their basic assumptions cause them to talk past each other rather than to engage in constructive dialogue.

THE "NATIONAL SECURITY ANALYST"

"National security" is not a phrase that enters into the everyday language of most people. But it is the subject with the highest priority in Washington. It covers a range of activities that are thought necessary to preserve the "American way of life," from the obvious requirements of defending the national territory to the promotion of U.S. prestige and the protection of American "interests" in various parts of the world. The definition of U.S. interests and of which ones are more "vital" than others is the job of the "national security analyst" in or out of government. As we will see, defining our "interests" in Central America is the most contested aspect of U.S. policy toward the region.

The "national security analyst" (or NSA) shares a set of assumptions with his or her colleagues. In the eyes of the NSA, defending the well-being of the United States is the highest duty any citizen can have and the greatest good. The protection of a country that stands for democracy, freedom, and prosperity is by its very nature a highly moral task.

The rub comes from the fact that the defense of the United States takes place in an amoral world. Nation-states, for the several hundred years they have existed, have engaged in the most heinous activities to protect themselves and to promote their own values. They are the foremost practitioners of the view that the end justifies the means. Among the means employed in the recent past have been genocide, sabotage, political assassination, and the bombing of civilian populations with conventional, chemical, and nuclear explosives.

DEFINING U.S. NATIONAL "INTERESTS"

The 167 countries of the world, whatever the nature of their economic or political systems, share the common foreign policy goal of protecting their "interests." "National interests" are those principles, beliefs, possessions, and practices that a nation will make commitments and sacrifices of varying intensity, short of war, to defend. "Vital interests" are those to which a nation will commit the maximum political, economic, and military resources.

A country's size, resources, location, and form of government help to determine how broadly its "interests" are defined. Small or weak powers may not be able even to defend their "vital interest" of protecting the national territory. Slightly larger, more powerful nations, such as Switzerland, may be willing to go to war only to repel attacks on their homeland and can be said to have few "interests" beyond their borders.

Great powers, or formerly great powers, define their interests more grandly. Britain, for example, was willing to go to war with Argentina to defend a few hundred British subjects on a small, barren island called the Falklands/Malvinas, located four thousand miles from England, near Antarctica.

The United States, the world's first superpower, endowed with enormous resources, has defined its interests more and more broadly since the Second World War. At various times it has viewed developments in any part of the world that diminished U.S. power or prestige as bearing on its national interests. The U.S. prime objective has been to prevent its strategic adversary, the Soviet Union, from dominating more countries than those over which it held sway at the end of the Second World War. To prevent the "loss" of countries to communism and to counter a presumed threat to its vital interests, the United States went to war in Korea (and won) and in Vietnam (and lost).

Since the promulgation of the Monroe Doctrine in 1823, the Caribbean Basin has been a special security interest of the United States. But after the last great imperial power, England, ended its presence in that region in the early twentieth century, the United States had no rivals in what came to be seen as its "sphere of influence." No threats to U.S. vital interests were seen as coming from the Caribbean Basin, and strategic priorities were focused elsewhere, primarily on the defense of Western Europe and Japan.

Now the creation of a Soviet ally in the region, Cuba, and developments in Grenada and Central America have raised security concerns for the United States in the Caribbean Basin. The classified U.S. Defense Guidance, the definitive statement of U.S. security interests around the world, ranks the defense of the Caribbean Basin (including Central America) on a par with the continental United States:

> The primary objective is to maintain the security of the North American Continent, the contiguous Caribbean Basin, and the sea and air approaches thereto (including Hawaii....
>
> [This section of the U.S. Defense Guidance was declassified for use in a paper by Colonel Nestor G. Pino-María, "The Strategic Importance of Central America for the United States," (Washington, D.C.: Washington Institute for Values in Public Policy, 1985).]

On the basis of this U.S. Defense Guidance, hostile developments in Central America would be defined as threatening "vital interests" of the United States.

As a result of the Vietnam conflict, domestic consensus about the definition of U.S. vital interests has broken down. HRAs argue that Vietnam demonstrated that the United States cannot and need not try to control events everywhere in the Third World. In an international system in which it is no longer the uniquely dominant power it once was, the United States must, HRAs believe, define its interests more modestly, husbanding scarce resources and uncertain public support for those crucial issues that can affect the well-being of its citizenry. The emergence of leftist regimes in the tiny countries of Central America is not, in the view of HRAs, such a crucial issue.

NSAs believe that the United States lacks only the political will to become the preeminent power it once was. The international system, they believe, requires one unifying, ordering power, and no country except the United States can play that role. As the ordering power, the United States must demonstrate its ability to control developments across the globe and, especially, in its strategic "backyard" of Central America.

These competing visions of U.S. "vital interests" are at the heart of disputes over U.S. policy toward Central America.

It is not surprising that, operating in the nasty world of nation-states, the NSA becomes cynical about the good that can be achieved in one's lifetime and impressed with humankind's capacity for evil. In this world of nation-states, the defense of the United States by means that in another context might seem suspect becomes acceptable and moral. The "real" world in which NSAs operate may require actions that would not normally be considered good or justifiable.

The relevance of this discussion to Central America is that the region has been defined by President Reagan and others as involving a "vital interest" of the United States—one for which U.S. citizens must be prepared to fight and die. So defined, Central America becomes for the NSA an area in which the end (defense of vital U.S. interests) justifies an extensive list of means (overthrowing governments, mining harbors, waging guerrilla warfare, etc.). If what happens in Central America is of "vital interest" to the United States, the "options list" of the NSA is limited basically by what the United States has the means to do, can gain the support of the public for, or can keep hidden from public view.

If you are made uncomfortable by the moral dilemmas inherent in the preceding paragraphs, you are not cut out to be an NSA.

THE "HUMAN RIGHTS ACTIVIST"

Somewhere on a different part of the political spectrum, another type of policy person can be found. "Human rights activists" (HRAs) have been involved in policy debates for far less time than NSAs. Their emergence roughly corresponds to the breakdown during the Vietnam years of the foreign-policy consensus that had endured since the Second World War. They too share certain assumptions about the way the world works and the role of U.S. policy in it.

A majority of the governments around the world, especially in the Third World and in the Socialist bloc, engage in systematic violations of human rights through physical and mental torture; illegal detention and prosecution; restriction of the rights of speech, assembly, association, and mobility; and other means. The HRA believes that the United States has an enviable, though imperfect, record of honoring human rights within its own borders and desires to extend those attitudes and practices to the rest of the world.

The HRA also believes, unlike the NSA, that the foreign policy of the United States should be formulated largely on the basis of respect for human rights. If other countries act in morally reprehensible ways by denying human rights, the best response of the United States is to denounce these abuses publicly and adopt policies designed to promote a climate of human-rights protection. The United States should hold out its behavior, based on respect for persons and for the principle of law, as the example that others should follow. The United States should virtually never look the other way or support governments that violate human rights without making a major issue of those violations. In the long run, HRAs argue, principled behavior, based on human rights as the cornerstone of U.S. foreign policy, will do the most to protect U.S. national security by encouraging more equitable, responsive governments and, hence, a more peaceful world.

If a foreign policy determined largely by human rights considerations appears a bit naive to you, then you are not cut out to be an HRA.

NSAs AND HRAs: THE DIFFICULT DIALOGUE

NSAs are usually in power in Washington and HRAs out of power, but not always. During the Carter administration many HRAs, or those substantially agreeing with the HRAs' perspectives on the world, were in positions of power. They frequently clashed with NSAs in the administration and in the career bureaucracy who did not share the same assumptions about the conduct of U.S. foreign policy. This made for the worst of both worlds: HRAs announced new policies, NSAs stalled on implementing them, and the rest of the world became confused. The Iranian hostage crisis and the Soviet invasion of

Afghanistan intervened to resolve this incongruity by making the world look so nasty that NSAs were put back in the saddle again. With the advent of the Reagan administration, the HRAs returned to their customary positions outside of power. What influence they exercise today is largely through the pressure they can mobilize on Congress.

In the following discussion of policies toward the five countries of Central America, and particularly with regard to the "hot topics" of El Salvador and Nicaragua, these stereotypical profiles of NSAs and HRAs can help to illuminate the policy debate. An illustration of how these two policy types engage each other is offered by the issue of U.S. support for the anti-Sandinista rebels fighting from bases in Honduras to overthrow the Nicaraguan government. The Sandinistas and HRAs call them *contras*, short for counterrevolutionaries; the president and NSAs call them freedom fighters, or democratic resistance fighters, comparable to the founding fathers of the United States. In a program on the Roosevelt Center's "American Debate" television series, then-Assistant Secretary for Inter-American Affairs Langhorne A. Motley and Congressman Bob Edgar (D-Pennsylvania) clashed over continued U.S. support for the rebels. An ordained Methodist minister, Congressman Edgar recounted to Secretary Motley the eyewitness accounts he had heard from church officials about *contra* atrocities:

"...I've been concerned that our policy basically has been to support the *contras* against the government of Nicaragua without any criticism of the brutality and terrorism of that particular organization. I'm a minister by vocation and a Congressman by accident. And over the last several months I've talked to people who are part of a number of groups who have gone to the border country, who have seen the atrocities of the *contras* and I am firmly convinced that our policy toward Nicaragua is a flawed policy....Our policy is morally indefensible. It's militarily stupid. And I don't think it is in the best interests of our government."

Secretary Motley replied:

"...You can expect in any kind of conflict atrocities, casualties. I noticed that you didn't use Urbina, who was a (Nicaraguan) bayoneted by the Sandinistas, taken out of the Costa Rican Embassy, a *cause célèbre* in the last two months. You didn't mention the young girl that's wandering around Washington now nine years old (whose parents were killed by the Sandinistas). For anybody to say that there aren't atrocities on either side, I think would be naive. That there are casualties in a war, I would agree with you."

If you think that Secretary Motley and Congressman Edgar are broadcasting on different wavelengths, you've just penetrated the first level of the policy debate inside Washington.

NICARAGUA

Question: Is the Sandinista Regime in Nicaragua a Threat to U.S. Interests in Central America?

Discussion: It is less than obvious to most North Americans how Nicaragua, a poor nation of less than 3 million people, could be a threat to a superpower like the United States. But for NSAs, Nicaragua represents a clear threat to the security of the region, to U.S. interests in the area, and, ultimately, to the national security of the United States itself.

The first way in which NSAs consider Nicaragua a threat to U.S. interests is the obvious case in which Nicaragua becomes a base for Soviet strategic forces—bombers or missiles that could attack the United States. The Soviet Union and the United States came to the brink of nuclear war when the Soviets attempted to place intermediate-range nuclear missiles in Cuba in 1962. In response, the Kennedy administration imposed a blockade of Cuba until Soviet leader Nikita Khrushchev agreed to the removal of the missiles. Kennedy, in turn, pledged not to invade Cuba.

The United States has made it clear several times since 1962 that it will not tolerate the introduction of land-based strategic weapons into the hemisphere, and it is hard to imagine a rational Soviet leadership that would attempt such a step again. If it were to be tried, this would clearly constitute a change in the strategic position of the superpowers and be considered a vital threat to the United States. Of course, with its missile-bearing submarines (which are serviced in Cuba), stationed off the coasts of the United States, the Soviet Union already has nuclear warheads closer to our borders than basing in Nicaragua would provide. However, the addition of land-based missiles or bombers in Nicaragua would be a dramatic escalation of the Soviet presence in the area and, in the minds of most North Americans, constitute a threat to our vital interests.

The "MIG scare" at the end of 1984 raised a second way in which Nicaragua could be viewed as a threat to the vital interests of the United States. MIG 21's, more modern aircraft than those possessed by other Central American countries, were thought to be on their way to Nicaragua aboard Soviet ships. Not a direct threat to U.S. territory, the aircraft could nevertheless change the regional balance of power between Nicaragua and her neighbors, particularly Honduras and Costa Rica. If Nicaragua were to attack her neighbors, the United States and other Latin American countries would be obligated by a 1947 treaty to come to the aid of the country under attack.

NSAs also view the MIGs as a more direct threat to the Caribbean waterways, called strategic lanes of communications (or SLOCs), through which 45 percent of U.S. foreign trade is shipped, 55 percent of U.S. crude oil imports pass, and 60 percent of supplies and reinforcements for a war in Europe or the Middle East would flow. The stationing of attack aircraft in Nicaragua would complement even more advanced planes already in Cuba and pose a potential threat to U.S. shipping in the event of certain kinds of limited conventional warfare. This is a situation which any reasonable military/strategic planner would like to avoid.

You may wonder how a nuclear superpower could be militarily preoccupied about attacks from small states in Central America and the Caribbean. Certainly war with the United States would be virtual suicide for the governments of Nicaragua or Cuba.

But NSAs are concerned about keeping as many options open as possible. Traditionally, the Caribbean Basin has been an area about which the United States did not need to be militarily concerned. This left military strategists free to allocate resources to other parts of the globe. The NSA sees a possibly hostile Nicaragua, linked to a small but tough Cuba (and, at one point, Grenada as well), as tying down the United States in an area that previously was of little concern to the military strategists. In their publication *The Soviet-Cuban Connection in Central America and the Caribbean* (March 1985), the departments of State and Defense argued the issue this way:

> The Soviet Union sees in the region an excellent and low-cost opportunity to preoccupy the United States—the "main adversary" of Soviet strategy—thus gaining greater freedom of action for the Soviet Union. While the Soviets are not likely to mount a direct military challenge to the United States in the Caribbean Basin, they are attempting to foment as much unrest as possible in an area that is at the strategic crossroads of the Western Hemisphere. Working through its key proxy in the region, Cuba, the Soviet Union hopes to force the United States to direct attention and military resources to an area that has not been a serious security concern to the United States in the past. [p.2]

For the NSA, the mere possession of advanced fighter craft or perhaps other weapons that could be considered offensive rather than defensive is a threat to the interests of the United States.

The last way in which Nicaragua could be a threat to the United States is by its very nature as a so-called Marxist-Leninist state. There is still a debate among well-informed people about whether the predominance of Marxist-Leninists in the Sandinista government and their increasing alignment with Cuba and the Soviet Union puts Nicaragua in the category of states such as Cuba or countries in the Eastern bloc. And regardless of what eventually happens in Nicaragua, analysts will argue about whether policies of the present or previous administrations pushed Nicaragua unnecessarily in the direction of the Soviet camp. But, for many, Nicaragua is already a Marxist-Leninist state in the Soviet orbit and, by its nature, constitutes a threat to U.S. interests. The reason is that Marxism-Leninism is said to be intrinsically expansionist and hence a threat to its neighbors either directly through attack or indirectly through subversion. Even if it never acquired a single MIG or installed Soviet missiles, Nicaragua would, according to this argument, constitute a threat to U.S. interests because of its desire to export revolution throughout the hemisphere.

This, of course, is the famous "domino theory" of Vietnam-era fame applied to Central America. In Central America, the domino theory works like this: Nicaragua becomes or already is a Marxist-Leninist state; little Nicaragua itself is not a threat to the United States, but Marxist-Leninist states are inherently expansionist and will subvert their neighbors, some of whom may fall to Marxism-Leninism themselves; a Marxist-Leninist Central America is a threat to more important countries in South America or to Mexico, a major supplier of oil to the United States that shares a two-thousand-mile border with us. Trouble in a border country like Mexico will eventually spill over into the United States in the form of migrants, terrorism and the diversion of U.S. military force to defend a previously peaceful border. In other words, the domino theory says, today it may be Managua, but tomorrow Mexico City and the next day El Paso or Los Angeles.

From the perspective of the domino theory, the United States needs to be concerned about the character of regimes in Central America and impose limits—by diplomacy if possible, by force if necessary—on what the United States considers to be acceptable governments in the region. Small countries such as those in Central America or even larger ones such as Mexico or Venezuela do not have the option of imposing limits on their neighbors, but the United States does. And in the nasty world of global power rivalries, NSAs argue, the United States needs to exercise that option to defend its own interests.

NSAs believe that U.S. responses to challenges in the Caribbean Basin will have a powerful impact on how other nations, particularly our allies and the Soviet Union, view the resolve of the United States. NSAs fear that if we are either unable or unwilling to control events close to home, our allies in Western Europe and the Third World will question our commitment to them. Furthermore, if the Soviet Union receives the message that the United States will not deter Soviet advances in a region so close to our borders, it may be tempted to test the United States in other parts of the world.

In discussing the ways in which Nicaragua could be seen as a threat to U.S. interests in Central America, we have gone from the fairly clear-cut case of a potential strategic threat from nuclear weapons to the much more murky threat posed by the "domino theory." Among experts and the general public, support for U.S. military action to defend our perceived interests roughly parallels the nature of the threat: there is great consensus about the correctness of the use of force to prevent the installation of missiles, for example; much less about using force to change the character of a regime.

HRAs who criticize U.S. hostility toward Nicaragua are often astounded at how exercised the leaders of the most powerful country in the world are about a poor nation of less than three million people such as Nicaragua. Some accuse the United States of formulating foreign policy on the basis of a national *insecurity* that the United States is experiencing as Central America pursues a more independent course.

Like NSAs, HRAs draw a line at the introduction of strategic nuclear weapons into Central America by an outside power. They would seek to prevent such a development by making a clear public statement to the Soviet Union that land-based nuclear weapons would not be tolerated in the hemisphere. An accommodation with Nicaragua that would remove fear of the United States as a motivation or pretext for military steps on the part of the Sandinistas would also be sought.

HRAs tend to focus on the ways in which the United States is a threat to Nicaragua and explain the military buildup that has occurred as being a response to U.S. hostility. While NSAs talk about MIGs and Hind-24 attack helicopters, HRAs criticize U.S. support for the *contras* as illegal, immoral, and counterproductive. They believe it has forced the Sandinistas to put more emphasis on military preparedness than would otherwise be the case. When NSAs point out that Nicaragua's buildup began before serious *contra* activities had been initiated, HRAs argue that, given the historical record, any revolutionary regime such as the Sandinistas has had to anticipate a hostile U.S. response at some point. Some military preparation is necessary to raise the costs of a possible U.S. intervention. To the extent that HRAs accept that the United States has legitimate security concerns about military developments in Nicaragua, they believe that these should be dealt with through negotiation, not threats and intimidation.

The issue over which HRAs become the most outraged is the "domino theory." They deny that the emergence of communist regimes in Laos and Cambodia after the fall of South Vietnam confirms a domino theory. Revolution, as the product of particular political, economic, and social factors, cannot be exported to other countries, they argue.

The United States, HRAs note, has been particularly unable to predict which Latin American revolutions would be friends and which enemies of the United States. In Cuba, the Republican Eisenhower administration initially failed to oppose Fidel Castro who once in power became Moscow's greatest ally in the Western Hemisphere. In Mexico, the United States denounced the Mexican Revolution as a Bolshevik plot and intervened militarily to affect its outcome. Until the 1940s the United States railed against Mexican radicalism. Yet President Franklin Roosevelt's decision to ignore demands for reprisals against Mexico's nationalization of U.S. oil companies in the thirties and to reach an accommodation with Mexico helped to produce a stable and moderate Mexico and healthy U.S.-Mexican relations.

As a superpower, HRAs argue, the United States should become more relaxed about developments in its border region. It should promote policies to correct the poverty, hunger, disease, and inequality that foment revolution in Central America, make clear its unwillingness to allow outside powers such as the Soviet Union (or Cuba) to intervene, but let the power of U.S. markets, financial aid, cultural appeal, and democratic practices work its charm on regimes bent on rapid social change.

HRAs hesitate to call Nicaragua a communist regime. They recognize that there are dedicated Marxist-Leninists in the government. Yet they find the regime remarkably open six years after the Sandinistas came to power compared to Cuba only two years after its revolution or, indeed, compared to noncommunist, authoritarian regimes in other parts of Central and Latin America to which the United States is much less hostile.

But HRAs also believe that Nicaragua has a right to any type of regime its people choose, even Marxist-Leninist. Just as a radical Nicaragua should be prevented from intervening in the affairs of its neighbors, so too the United States must refrain from attempting to impose its preferred system, democratic or not, on the Nicaraguans.

NSAs don't believe that a Marxist-Leninist regime is ever freely chosen but that it is rather imposed on an unwilling population. HRAs are not so sure. They view the obvious popularity of the Sandinistas after their triumph in 1979 as confirmation of the legitimacy of the government. They emphasize the health-care, literacy, and land-reform programs enacted during the early years of the Sandinista government as evidence of commitments to the common people of the country. The much-disputed election of 1984, while flawed, is taken by HRAs as further confirmation of Sandinista legitimacy and commitment to some forms of political dissent. As with elections in other Latin countries, notably El Salvador, elections including a broader spectrum of political views could be imagined. For HRAs, new elections in Nicaragua might be desirable as part of some future political accord, but the 1984 Nicaraguan elections should not be condemned as totally fraudulent.

NSAs counter each one of these conclusions by HRAs. Their specific rejoinders can be found in a series of documents and analyses published by the State Department's Office of Public Diplomacy for Latin America and the Caribbean.[1] But the bottom line for NSAs is that the leaders of Nicaragua are Marxist-Leninists who will do or say anything to achieve their ultimate objective: domination of Nicaragua by a single party and alignment with Cuba and the Soviet Union. With this as their objective, there is little that the United States can do through negotiations or greater understanding to change Nicaragua's course. By its very nature, the NSAs say, a Sandinista Nicaragua constitutes a threat to the United States which must be faced.

Question: Does a Policy of Military and Economic Pressure on Nicaragua have the Best Chance of Influencing the Sandinistas to Become More Democratic and Less Menacing to their Neighbors?

Discussion: In a February 21, 1985, news conference, President Reagan stated more clearly than before his belief that the goal of U.S. policy in Nicaragua must be to "change the character" of the Sandinista regime. The specific exchange is worth quoting:

> **Question:** Mr. President, on Capitol Hill the other day [the] Secretary of State suggested that the goal of your policy now is to remove the Sandinista government in Nicaragua. Is that your goal?
>
> **Answer:** Well, remove it in the sense of its present structure, in which it is a communist, totalitarian state and it is not a government chosen by its people....
>
> * * *
>
> **Question:** To the question, aren't you advocating the overthrow of the present government, if not to substitute another form of what you say was the revolution?
>
> **Answer:** Not if the present government would turn around and say—all right—if they'd say uncle, or all right, and come back over into the revolutionary government and let's straighten this out and institute the goals.

Although there are legal and diplomatic reasons why a president of one country cannot publicly call for the overthrow of another legally recognized government, President Reagan came about as close as one can come to doing so. Perhaps the best way to sum up the president's statement is to say that, in his view, the Sandinista leopard must either change its spots or go.

NSAs point to statements by the Sandinistas that betray them as dedicated Marxist-Leninists who, by definition, will never accept true democracy. They cite a secret speech made in the spring of 1984 to the Nicaraguan Socialist party (PSN), a Moscow-line communist party, by Sandinista National Directorate member and political coordinator Bayardo Arce acknowledging that the FSLN (Sandinista National Liberation Front) had never intended to comply with its promises to promote pluralism, a mixed economy, and nonalignment. In the speech, Arce explained that the FSLN had made these commitments simply to gain international support and thereby forestall possible U.S. intervention. For NSAs this is the real intent of the Sandinistas.

It is not a meaningless question, then, whether U.S. support for anti-Sandinista rebels, military maneuvers in Honduras, economic reprisals and other measures are designed to pressure the Sandinistas into making concessions but still leave them in power, or to create conditions that will fuel internal dissent and, when combined with *contra* activities, lead to the overthrow of the Sandinista government.

A policy of pressure against the Sandinistas such as that recommended by NSAs has both positive and negative effects. NSAs emphasize the positive outcomes, HRAs the negative ones. For example, the U.S.-supported warfare on Nicaragua's borders with Honduras and Costa Rica has had both positive and negative effects on Nicaragua from the point of view of the stated objectives of U.S. policy. Nicaragua has taken steps typical of a country on a war footing: initiated a draft, militarized the society, limited dissent and the operation of a free press, and stigmatized the legitimate opposition as linked to the "treasonous" rebels. This reduction in domestic political freedom, which began before the *contras* received CIA support, can be justified by the Sandinistas as a response to the military pressure of the *contra* war. Economic dislocations caused in part by Sandinista mistakes as well as by economic sabotage can be blamed entirely on "Yankee aggression." HRAs emphasize that the most radical elements of the Sandinista leadership are strengthened politically against more moderate elements by the pressure from the United States. (Of course, these "negative" consequences are "positive" if the aim of U.S. policy is to make conditions so bad politically and economically that internal dissent leads to the overthrow of the regime and the installation of a new, and presumably better, replacement.)

The pressure also appears to have had "positive" results. Many NSAs and HRAs agree that the November 1984 elections were held by the Sandinistas in an attempt to relegitimize the government in Latin American and European eyes and to counteract U.S. hostility. *La Prensa*, the stridently anti-Sandinista newspaper that has become a symbol of press freedom to the outside world, would probably be more effectively harassed or shut down by the Sandinistas if external pressure to preserve it did not exist.

Former Assistant Secretary Motley made the case for pressuring the Sandinistas succinctly and effectively in testimony to the Subcommittee on Western Hemisphere Affairs of the House Foreign Affairs Committee in early 1985:

- The Sandinistas have global ties and plans for Nicaragua and the rest of Central America that are contrary to U.S. interests;

- They will not modify or bargain over their position until there is some incentive for them to do so;

- The only incentive that has proved effective thus far has been opposition from other Nicaraguans;

- If pressure is taken away, the Sandinistas will have no reason to compromise;

- If the Sandinistas have no reason to compromise, Contadora will surely fail; and

- If Contadora fails, the long-run costs to the United States in terms of money and lives will be much greater.
  [*Current Policy* #655, p.7]

CONTADORA: A CAT WITH NINE LIVES

In January 1983, representatives of four Latin American countries met on a resort island off the coast of Panama to discuss what they could do collectively about the Central American crisis. Mexico, Colombia, Panama, and Venezuela each had different perspectives on and relations with key countries in Central America, but all had a common interest in deterring unilateral action by the United States in the region and in seeking a negotiated solution to conflicts within and among the Central American countries.

As a student of the Contadora process has noted, this regional initiative is, like motherhood and apple pie, rhetorically supported by all parties to the Central American conflict. Yet Contadora has yet to reach its objective of obtaining a peaceful settlement and has appeared at times to be completely ignored or contradicted by important actors in the region. Why?

The key to understanding Contadora lies in understanding the nature of a process of negotiation. From its beginnings, Contadora accepted the idea that its role was to achieve a balance among *all* the forces at work in the region. That meant giving some concessions to the Sandinista government, its external opposition, the Duarte government and its guerrilla opposition, the fears of Nicaragua about the United States, and, to a lesser extent, the fears of the United States and certain Central American countries about the Sandinistas. Contadora can make progress only to the degree that the main parties to the conflicts in the region, the Central American countries and the United States, are willing to accept such concessions. As time has passed since January 1983, different actors have at different times and for different reasons been unwilling to concede ground to their adversaries.

In 1985 the main stumbling block to concessions became Nicaragua. Contadora, by its very nature, was designed to leave the Sandinistas in power, while creating agreements through treaty backed by international supervision that would protect the other Central American countries from Nicaragua and Nicaragua from the United States. As it became clearer that the Reagan administration would never trust any Sandinista government to fulfill treaty commitments and that the Sandinistas would not voluntarily surrender power, Contadora foundered.

Among the Contadora four, domestic changes have made cooperation more difficult. During 1985, Panama's first elected civilian president in 16 years was deposed by the military, and Mexico held gubernatorial elections roundly condemned as fraudulent by the opposition. The irony of these two countries helping to bring democracy to Central America became too glaring to ignore. Mexico's increasing financial woes in late 1985 encouraged President de la Madrid to deemphasize Mexico's support for Nicaragua within Contadora in the hopes of greater flexibility on the part of the United States in debt renegotiations. Colombia and Venezuela, with less questionable democratic traditions, became increasingly concerned about Sandinista intentions themselves.

Among the Central American countries, Costa Rica moved closer to El Salvador and Honduras, which had always been skeptical of the Sandinistas, when border conflicts with Nicaragua increased in the last half of 1985. Guatemala was less hostile to Nicaragua publicly, in part to gain Mexico's cooperation in dealing with guerrillas operating out of Guatemalan refugee camps in Mexico, but was said privately to be equally worried about the Sandinistas.

Contadora reached a new stalemate in December 1985 when pressures built to sign a revised draft treaty that reflected U.S. concerns about Nicaragua and strengthened enforcement provisions from previous drafts. Nicaragua was forced to call for a six-month suspension of the talks to avoid rejecting outright a draft treaty it could not accept.

Perceived as the only alternative to direct intervention by the United States or to a regional war, Contadora has been counted out many times only to revive itself again. Such a development occurred in the summer of 1985 when the so-called Lima Group of Peru, Brazil, Argentina and Uruguay lent their support to Contadora as a counterweight to the increasing hostility between the United States and Nicaragua. Yet as long as any of the central actors (the United States, the Sandinistas, the *contras*, the Salvadoran government, the FMLN guerrillas) holds out a hope for achieving its maximum objectives without making significant concessions to its adversary, Contadora cannot succeed. Contadora may be a cat with nine lives. But it has already died seven times.

NSAs advocate such a policy of "coercive diplomacy"—ratcheting up the pressure on a diplomatic adversary to obtain agreement on certain clear objectives—against Nicaragua. Every president, they argue, has engaged in such tactics at one time or another. The stated objectives of the "coercive diplomacy" toward Nicaragua are to force the Sandinistas to comply with their supposed commitment to the Organization of American States to support democratic pluralism and to respect human and civil rights, to reduce the size of Nicaragua's military force, to cut Nicaraguan military and security ties to Cuba and the Soviet bloc, and to end Nicaraguan support for guerrilla groups in neighboring countries.

HRAs are concerned, however, that if the Sandinistas are the confirmed Marxist-Leninists that NSAs say they are, they will never be willing to accept these conditions. At some point, additional pressure will no longer lead to further concessions on the Sandinistas' part but to the conviction that no response is acceptable but capitulation. At that point the Sandinistas may decide to harden their position. Like other revolutionaries before them, they might rather die a martyr's death than let history judge that they sacrificed their principles. They could even "welcome" a U.S. invasion as a vindication of all they have said about the evil intentions of the United States.[2]

NSAs emphasize the necessity for power and strength in any diplomatic encounter. They rely on U.S. military assets to play a large role in persuading opponents to accept agreements they might otherwise resist. HRAs believe in the peaceful resolution of disputes as a principle. Agreements are likely to endure, they argue, only if they are the result of mutual concessions.

HRAs suspect the true objectives of the United States in Nicaragua are the overthrow of a radical experiment in social change that might both prosper and be less threatening to the United States if it were faced with less hostility. NSAs suspect the real goal of the Sandinistas is a Marxist-Leninist state after the fashion of the Soviet Union and Cuba. Left alone, Nicaragua would become a source of irritation if not mortal danger to her neighbors and, through them, ultimately to the United States.

EL SALVADOR

Question: Is the Conflict in El Salvador the Result of Political, Economic, and Social Problems or a Textbook Case of Indirect Armed Aggression by Communist Powers Through Cuba?

Discussion: There is a little-publicized debate raging in Washington over whether Central America should be defined as an East-West or a North-South problem. East-West problems are usually considered the cream of international issues, the ones that directly affect relations between the superpowers. Nuclear war, the security of Western Europe, the balance of strategic weapons—these are all examples of issues that influence the basic balance between the Soviet Union and the United States; a balance that has kept us at "cold war" for forty years but has also prevented either of the superpowers from risking an attack on its rival. For NSAs, East-West issues are the "sexiest" of all policy issues because they concern the basic survival of the United States.

North-South issues deal instead with relations between the often newly independent states of the Third World (largely located south of the equator) and the wealthy, industrial, capitalist powers of the North. The North includes the older "imperial" powers of Europe, whose former colonies now constitute the Third World, and the United States, which had few colonial possessions but is viewed as the new "imperial" power of the post-Second World War era by many in the South. North-South issues generally concern economic questions such as trade, investment, and aid and usually involve demands by the South for assistance in their drive for improved standards of living. The issues also have political and social dimensions, as much of the Third World is still struggling to create representative political institutions and to integrate regional, ethnic, or racial divisions into a national whole.

Defining the problems of Central America as North-South is to assert that the conflicts stem from the political, economic, and social problems common to the less-developed countries of the world. Central America is one of the poorest parts of Latin America, and there are great gaps there between the poor majority and the wealthy few, who have ruled the region for decades. To argue that Central America is a North-South issue is to assert that the challenges to the United States in the region stem from social, economic, and political causes indigenous to the region and that our response should primarily address these causes by supporting progressive social reform and promoting governments that are responsive to the needs of the majority.

To assert that Central America is an East-West issue is to focus on the Soviet Union (and its presumed instruments, Cuba and Nicaragua) as the source of problems in the region. President Reagan, for example, stated in a 1980 campaign interview that there would be no hot spots in the world were not the Soviet Union behind them. Expressed in this bald a fashion, the East-West optic sees all trouble for the United States in the world as stemming from Soviet (or other) communist machinations and not from indigenous developments or, for that matter, from problems that the United States had a hand in creating. Viewing an issue from an East-West perspective also defines it as a zero-sum game in which any advance by one side implies a loss by the other. To the extent that Central America is an East-West problem, the United States must become involved if for no other reason than to prevent a gain by the Soviet Union.

Few NSAs or HRAs view Central America as exclusively an East-West or a North-South problem, but there are important differences in emphasis between our two stereotypical policy types that have significant implications for future policy.

NSAs stress military aid as only one part of a much larger program of economic assistance and social reform in Central America designed to address the acknowledged North-South dimension of the problems. They insist, however, on the need for a military "shield" to protect the U.S. investment in economic and democratic development from communist attack and to allow this assistance to have effect. Marxist-Leninists, they argue, want to take advantage of local injustices and to use the population's anger to impose a new dictatorship that not only fails to address the injustices but imposes new tyrannies on an unwilling population. Communism, by definition, cannot be a freely chosen form of government for a nation; it is always imposed. Unless the military shield is there to protect a government under attack, no amount of reform will satisfy communist guerrillas bent on the installation of their dictatorship.

HRAs hold the United States responsible for neglecting, if not causing, many of Central America's problems. They note the appearance of effective leftist guerrillas in the region only after earlier attempts at reform had been thwarted by local elites solely concerned with the protection of their own privileged positions. They lament the short-sightedness of the United States in ignoring social problems and supporting groups opposed to any change. In the past, argue HRAs, in countries such as Mexico and Guatemala, the United States' fear of communism led it to oppose true reformist movements that were mild compared to what the United States itself now tries to impose in countries such as El Salvador. Unless the United States remains focused primarily on the indigenous origins of the region's problems, it is likely to lose its way politically, choose the stability of a conservative regime over necessary change as it has done so often in the past, and encourage more radical and threatening developments in the future.

HRAs emphasize the historical amnesia that afflicts much of the policy-making community in Washington. They wonder, given the historical record, how long-term the commitment of some NSAs to reform would be if, magically, Soviet-Cuban sponsored insurgents were to disappear from Central America overnight. Given their emphasis on the external dimension of the Central American crisis, HRAs ask whether NSAs can be trusted to choose reform over stability in the day-to-day decisions required by the fluid and dynamic process occurring in El Salvador. Will the United States desert President Duarte, so far to the left ideologically from many NSAs, if the situation stabilizes sufficiently to permit a less reform-minded alternative to Duarte?

HRAs charge that NSAs tend to forget past behavior that contributed to current dilemmas and to overreact to movements for social change. HRAs are in turn criticized by NSAs for seeming to ignore the changing realities of a better-armed and more active Cuba and of a Soviet Union more able than ever before to project its power far from its shores. Cuba did not create the problems in Central America nor, in most cases, the guerrilla forces that have arisen in the region. But, argue NSAs, it has played a crucial role at critical points in providing basic military training for many of the guerrilla leaders and in coordinating unified "fronts" of diverse guerrilla factions that proved more effective in waging war. It has never been easy to make true revolution anywhere in Latin America. However, the presence of Cuba is increasingly helping to change the balance of forces between those opposed to change, those supporting democratic reform, and those dedicated to the violent overthrow of the old system.

Some HRAs argue that emphasizing the North-South aspect of Central America's problems is, in fact, the best way for the United States to score points in the East-West game. They point out that the Soviet Union has very limited ability to offer what Third World countries need most—trade, aid, technology, markets. Let radical regimes in Latin America rant at the United States if they must. Eventually, if the United States shows forebearance, these regimes will come to recognize that the United States has too much to offer to be ignored or made the object of long-term hostility.

Whatever such an approach to radical change in Latin America might have to recommend it, NSAs argue that such a program could face some short-term political realities that would prohibit its being tried long enough to work. They point out that although the Soviet Union has limited economic and financial assistance to offer Third World countries, it does have something that can be of immediate and often decisive help: military aid. Directly or through Cuba or other allies, the Soviet Union can and has delivered the firepower (and, at times, the Cuban troops) that has made the difference. The problems of governing, once power is achieved, may incline a new regime more toward the United States, but the earlier Soviet military aid at a moment of crisis gets the Soviets in on the ground floor of many new radical regimes.

The historical legacy of the United States in Latin America also weighs heavily in the competition for the affections of radical regimes. For many in Latin America, not only the left, it is the United States, not the Soviet Union, that has historically constituted a threat to their countries. Because of its historic dominance of the region, the United States would probably be resented by its weaker and poorer Latin American neighbors even if its past behavior had been a model of relations between big and small powers. The United States was not, of course, such a model.

The United States can expect, then, to be viewed skeptically, if not with outright hostility, by left-of-center governments in Latin America. It may have to endure years of venomous rhetoric and actions designed to show a new radical regime's independence of and contempt for "Yankee imperialism." Relations with Cuba and the Soviet Union, if not already strong because of past military help and ideological affinities, will be developed to act as a counterweight to the power of the United States in the hemisphere. Indeed, these ties will be sought precisely because they are the one sore point through which the new government can have some impact on Washington.

The policy recommendation of HRAs that the United States be the "faithful suitor" of leftist regimes in Latin America calls for a great deal of patience on the part of U.S. leaders and the general public. The political difficulties of maintaining a policy that seems rewarded only with anti-U.S. rhetoric and actions are formidable.

NSAs point out that such a policy toward the revolution in Nicaragua was, in fact, tried and ran into these difficulties. After great ambivalence on the part of the Carter administration toward the ouster of Somoza, the United States offered a generous aid package to the Sandinistas and exercised forbearance in the hope that the hostile rhetoric would eventually diminish and not lead to actions inimical to U.S. interests. Aid was finally suspended when it became clear to the Carter administration that the Sandinistas were significantly aiding the Salvadoran guerrillas. Carter's ambassador to Nicaragua, Lawrence Pezzullo, argues that his strong criticism of the arms flow to the guerrillas resulted in a cutback and that such a carrot-and-stick policy toward the Sandinistas would have worked to moderate the regime over time. He was never proven right or wrong because the Reagan administration canceled the aid package in April 1981 and pursued a stick-and-stick policy toward Nicaragua thereafter. NSAs question whether even the Carter administration could have sustained the carrot-and-stick approach over the years, not just months, that might have been required to moderate and contain the Sandinista revolution. Would political support in the Congress and among the public have been there even if Carter were reelected?

Question: Should the United States Assist the Salvadoran Government to Win the War Against the Leftist Guerrillas Militarily or Urge the Government to Seek Some Form of Negotiated Settlement?

Discussion: The war in El Salvador has been going on since 1979. Perhaps as many as 60,000 lives have been lost, the majority of them civilians rather than soldiers or guerrillas. As a result of the violence, nearly 10 percent of El Salvador's population of 5 million have been driven into internal or external exile. It would seem evident that an end to the conflict would be most people's top priority, and it is. But opinions differ widely about how to achieve real and enduring peace in El Salvador.

One option no longer seriously discussed by either NSAs or HRAs is that chosen by the United States in Vietnam: withdrawal. Most observers believe that withdrawal of support by the United States would result in a victory by the left. Some HRAs, persuaded of the good intentions of the guerrillas and of their civilian political allies, see the establishment of a leftist government dedicated to reform and social justice as producing stability in El Salvador.

NSAs, who view the guerrillas and their supporters as Marxist-Leninists, see a leftist victory as the first in a series of destabilizing losses that could enflame the entire region. El Salvador itself might be pacified under a totalitarian system but its revolutionary government would try to extend its radical politics beyond its borders in cooperation or perhaps even in competition with neighboring Nicaragua. In line with the domino theory, NSAs argue, victory for the left in El Salvador would be the beginning, not the end, of conflict in the region and of security threats to the United States.

A second option advocated by some NSAs but not an officially declared goal of the United States is military victory[3] by the Salvadoran government. In this option, diplomatic negotiations can be part of an overall strategy for defeating the guerrillas but cannot replace military victory as the ultimate goal of U.S. policy. Otherwise, anti-U.S. guerrilla forces will feel free to wage armed subversion in pursuit of military victory without risking ultimate defeat or destruction. Should their circumstances become desperate, they can try to negotiate a settlement with the United States that leaves them in a position to subvert from within or to return to a guerrilla strategy when conditions permit a change in tactics.

HRAs counter that the price of military victory will be high, if it can be achieved. Official estimates are that there are roughly 6,000 to 8,000 guerrillas. To achieve a military victory, most of these actual fighters would need to be killed, captured, or forced to surrender or to leave the country. In addition, it is estimated that for every guerrilla fighter there are roughly three to ten *masas*, or civilian supporters, of the guerrillas. Some of the 18,000 to 80,000 *masas* would undoubtedly desert a losing guerrilla cause. But other passive or active supporters of the guerrillas, now branded as "subversives," would face the same fate as the guerrillas.

To achieve military victory, the Salvadoran armed forces might need to be increased beyond their present size of a little over 40,000 men. A ratio used in classic discussions of guerrilla warfare is that to defeat a guerrilla army, a conventional army must outnumber it by ten to one. If this ratio were to hold in El Salvador, the Salvadoran army might need to more than double its present size. This would entail the obvious economic expenditures by El Salvador (and, indirectly, by the United States) for training, salaries, and equipment. U.S. economic and military assistance well beyond the $1.5 billion provided since 1981 would be required. In addition, there are the difficult-to-calculate political costs to El Salvador's fledgling democratic institutions of its armed forces growing to nearly twice their present size, given a history of military intervention in politics. At least one of El Salvador's neighbors, Honduras, already feels threatened by the size of the well-equipped Salvadoran army, having fought a "Soccer War" with El Salvador in 1969.

An all-out effort to defeat the guerrillas militarily will also exact a price in civilian casualties. The kind of counterinsurgency warfare involving "model villages," "free-fire" zones, and the use of aerial bombing that the Salvadoran armed forces must employ to try to win the war, has traditionally had a high cost in civilian casualties.

There are too many variables to make a reliable calculation of the human costs of an attempt to win a military victory in El Salvador. Some NSAs believe that a victory drive by the Salvadoran armed forces with the full backing and funding of the United States would lead to a precipitous collapse of the guerrilla forces. HRAs believe that such massive violence by the government would radicalize the civilian population and lead to greater support for the guerrillas. All agree that tens of thousands of lives would be lost in the struggle.

NSAs, convinced that the Soviet Union is orchestrating a strategy for eventual domination of the hemisphere, see these costs as acceptable if, as a result of their military defeat in El Salvador, the communists are dissuaded from attempting armed subversion elsewhere. In this grey area between ideological competition and all-out war, where communist forces are seen as having an advantage, the United States would have demonstrated, as it did not in Vietnam, that it can defeat guerrilla forces at their own game. For those who view El Salvador in these terms, almost any cost would be worthwhile in order to deliver such a setback to the communists' global strategy.

For HRAs the pursuit of military victory in El Salvador would be a disaster on a scale unprecedented since Vietnam. Aside from the costs to El Salvador in lives lost on all sides, the drive toward military victory could reopen wounds in the U.S. body politic that are just now beginning to heal. Escalating warfare costing tens of thousands of lives that was a direct outcome of U.S. policy could well, in the view of HRAs, reignite the protests and internal divisions of the Vietnam era even if carried out by the Salvadorans themselves. If, however, the Salvadoran army faltered and the United States assumed a direct combat role—a possibility if not a probability—severe domestic repercussions would result. The recently achieved consensus to rebuild U.S. forces vis-à-vis the Soviet Union could be undermined, valuable strategic resources from other parts of the world would be diverted to the traditionally low-priority area of the Caribbean Basin, and anti-U.S. sentiment in Latin America boosted at a time when the emergence of new democracies there had given hope for better hemispheric relations. Before it had time to develop a new consensus about its role in the Third World in the post-Iran and post-Afghanistan era, the United States would be plunged into another conflict whose casualties and refugees would make themselves felt directly at home.

IS EL SALVADOR SPANISH FOR VIETNAM?

Adviser—Vietnam-era term for Trainer (See **Trainer**).
Trainer—Central America-era term for Adviser.
  —"Salvospeak," *Soldier of Fortune*
  magazine (March 1985).

As U.S. involvement in El Salvador has increased, many HRAs have tried to draw analogies between El Salvador and Vietnam. The object of the analogies, of course, is to alarm public opinion by suggesting that the United States is taking the same course pursued in Vietnam with such disastrous results: more than 50,000 dead, the first U.S. military defeat in modern times, the "loss" of Vietnam, Laos, and Cambodia to communism, and fractures in our domestic social fabric that continue to the present.

As in other debates over Central America, those who argue for and against comparing El Salvador to Vietnam are usually talking past each other. When they raise the specter of Vietnam, most HRAs are suggesting that the United States is entering another conflict, without understanding its fundamental nature, that has the potential to divide American public opinion and undermine confidence in the nation's institutions. For HRAs, Vietnam was a local conflict in which the United States should not have become involved or should have tried to solve by diplomatic rather than military means. "Victory" in Vietnam was not possible at costs commensurate with the interests at stake for the United States.

For NSAs, Vietnam represents a defeat that the United States need not and should not have suffered. A noble effort, U.S. involvement in Vietnam was undermined by radical opposition in the United States and political leaders who restrained the military from devoting the resources necessary to win the battle. For NSAs, the war in Vietnam was lost in the streets, the U.S. media, and the White House, not on the battlefield. It should and could have been won.

When a reporter asked President Reagan in a March 1981 press conference if El Salvador could become another Vietnam and he replied that it could not because El Salvador is much closer to the United States and because the United States is not just aiding El Salvador but defending the entire Western Hemisphere from a takeover by communism, HRAs saw his response as a *non sequitur* or as a confirmation of their worst fears.

Former Assistant Secretary for Inter-American Affairs Motley has discussed the Vietnam analogy in a useful way. In testimony before the Subcommittee on Western Hemisphere Affairs of the House Foreign Affairs Committee in 1985, he said:

> There are two things that the vast majority of the American people do not want in this region so close to home: they do not want a second Cuba, and they do not want a second Vietnam. By a second Cuba, I mean the institionalization of another well-armed communist state, this time on the mainland, supported by the Soviet Union and working actively against U.S. interests and friends in the region. And, by a second Vietnam, I mean a prolonged conflict involving U.S. combat troops with no clear goal and no end in sight consistent with the protection of strategic American interests.
>
> It is true that some Americans are concerned with one and not the other: some would risk another Vietnam to prevent another Cuba, while others are so concerned with any sign of a second Vietnam that they ignore the threat of a second Cuba. But the majority of our fellow citizens seek and will support a policy which serves our interests while preventing both a new Cuba and a new Vietnam.

Secretary Motley is probably correct in arguing that the prevention of a new Cuba or a new Vietnam sets the limits for the broadest consensus on Central American policy. NSAs believe they are pursuing such a course by increasing assistance to the Salvadoran government and to the Nicaraguan rebels while limiting direct U.S. military involvement. If this strategy is as successful as NSAs believe it will be, another Cuba and another Vietnam would be prevented.

HRAs point out, however, that in their efforts to gain support for this policy, NSAs have defined the importance of Central America to the United States in increasingly dramatic terms. It is now seen as a vital interest of the United States and significant U.S. prestige has been attached to our ability to influence the outcome of events in the region. If the current policy of massive assistance and limited direct U.S. military support fails to defeat the Salvadoran guerrillas and unseat the Sandinistas, the United States will be faced with the option of accepting a blow to its prestige or escalating the level of direct U.S. commitment. This is precisely what happened in Vietnam. Each time the choice was faced the option of escalation was elected until the disintegration of support for the war at home forced withdrawal and even greater defeat for U.S. interests and prestige.

Thus, for HRAs, the verdict is still out on whether El Salvador is, as the bumper stickers say, Spanish for Vietnam.

A third possible path to peace in El Salvador is a negotiated solution that somehow reconciles the guerrillas and their supporters with the government and the army. There are few if any precedents for resolving a deeply divisive conflict like El Salvador's by negotiation. But faced with the costs of the alternatives—withdrawal or military victory—many HRAs look to a negotiated solution with hope.

How would a negotiated end to the war work? When President Duarte called for a dialogue with the guerrillas in 1984, there were undoubtedly some who hoped that a five-year war that had cost tens of thousands of lives could be settled merely by meetings and talks. More realistically, the recognition of each side implied by the face-to-face meeting was but the first step of a very long process of reconciliation that has the odds stacked against it.

The initial meetings between the guerrillas (the FMLN) and their political representatives (the FDR) and the Salvadoran government produced two sets of positions that have led to a stalemate. President Duarte argued on behalf of the government that the conditions of civil strife, repression, death squads, and military-dominated politics that had produced and perhaps justified the escalation of armed conflict in 1979 were now on their way to being removed. The process of reform and democratization represented by President Duarte was sufficiently under way for the FDR-FMLN to renounce armed struggle, accept the new constitution of 1984 drawn up by a Legislative Assembly dominated by the right wing and rejoin the political process as citizen participants. Essentially, this was a position that called on the guerrillas to admit that their costly fight was no longer justified and to accept that forces in the army and the death squads that had fought viciously against them were to become the guardians of their safe reintegration into civil society.

The guerrillas for their part demanded to be considered as a virtual government-in-exile. They refused to accept the rules of the political game set out in a 1984 constitution which they had had no part in developing. They called, therefore, for the delegitimization of the electoral process that had brought Duarte to power and the development of a new constitution, new elections, and a new army that would integrate the guerrilla fighters into the traditional armed forces.

These positions are irreconcilable. NSAs believe that the guerrillas, as Marxists, will never negotiate in good faith for a democratic solution and are not surprised that the guerrillas would propose unacceptable conditions. They urge the Salvadoran government to continue the talks for the sake of appearance while prosecuting the war to the fullest. HRAs argue, that these initial statements may only represent the opening of a bargaining process that will become more serious over time. Few expected that such negotiations would ever have occurred in the first place, but they did, due largely to President Duarte's forceful personality and vision of himself as the savior of his country. It is not inconceivable, HRAs argue, that future breakthroughs could occur.

HRAs believe that the future of the negotiations will be strongly affected by two central actors in El Salvador—the U.S. government and the Salvadoran military. Although supportive (after the fact) of Duarte's overtures to the guerrillas made in his speech to the United Nations on October 8, 1984, the United States seemed to many HRAs to be genuinely surprised by his bold step. HRAs are also made uneasy by the commitment of many NSAs to a military victory over the guerrillas that would "send a message" to other insurgency movements in the region and throughout the world. HRAs point out that most NSAs remain opposed to any type of "power-sharing" arrangement in which the guerrillas gain some form of participation in the government outside the framework of the present constitution.

NSAs insist that the guerrillas participate in elections, and they repeatedly state their aversion to the guerrillas "shooting their way into power." NSAs believe that "power sharing" would reward the guerrillas for their violent actions, encourage other groups to employ similar tactics, and, ultimately, be used by the guerrillas to subvert a democratic government from within.

A second key group limiting the possibility of negotiations is the Salvadoran military. There is a raging debate over the true nature of the Salvadoran military: are they reform-minded patriots or silent partners of the death squads? Both elements continue to coexist in the military and each has gained dominance at one point or another in Salvadoran history.

Minister of Defense General Vides Casanova, who accompanied President Duarte to the first peace talks in La Palma, and much of the high command are viewed as supporters of President Duarte, based on Duarte's ability to command respect abroad and to obtain the U.S. congressional funding essential to meet the country's economic and military needs. In the 1985 legislative elections from which Duarte's party emerged the surprising victor, the armed forces solidly opposed attempts by the losing right-wing parties to discredit the results of the elections. For his part, Duarte has gone to great lengths since coming to office to praise the military, exhort it to greater efforts against the guerrillas and to act as an effective commander-in-chief whom the armed forces can respect. (The concessions made by President Duarte to the guerrillas to obtain the release of his kidnapped daughter in November of 1985 were viewed by some as the first important threat to his support among the military.) As noted, his opening position in talks with the guerrillas offered few concessions that would upset the military.

A critical point will come, however, if the talks ever move beyond the irreconcilable stage at which they currently stand. Issues such as "power sharing" and a role for the guerrilla fighters in the nation's armed forces have the potential to cause deep divisions within the military. At this point, HRAs believe, the role of the United States will become crucial. The United States will have several tools at its disposal, such as linking future aid to the Salvadoran government and military to progress in the negotiations, that could support the negotiation process. Or it could frustrate negotiations by encouraging those politicians and military officers opposed to any agreement with the guerrillas. If such a moment arrives in the negotiations, the debate between NSAs and HRAs over whether to pursue military victory with its toll in human lives or the difficult and dangerous road of negotiations will decide the future of U.S. relations with El Salvador.

At this point, you are probably somewhat pessimistic about the future of El Salvador. The options of withdrawal and military victory have high costs, although military victory may be possible. Negotiations to produce a political settlement appear less costly in human terms but seem exceedingly difficult. The "options list" of the NSA and the HRA are relatively short and very problematic. There are no easy solutions. Meanwhile, the war drags on.

HONDURAS

Question: Does the U.S. Military Buildup in Honduras Serve U.S. Interests?

Discussion: Beginning in early 1984, the United States engaged in a large buildup of U.S. forces either temporarily or permanently staged in Honduras. Since 1983 there have been nine joint U.S.-Honduran military maneuvers, costing some $1 billion and each involving between 1,000 and 5,000 U.S. troops. "Temporary" installations have also been built and a regional military training center established to instruct Salvadoran and Honduran armed forces.

NSAs deny that the buildup in Honduras is out of the ordinary but admit that the maneuvers and other activities are part of a campaign of pressure against Nicaragua. HRAs charge that the buildup has converted Honduras into a virtual land-bound aircraft carrier poised on Nicaragua's border to intimidate and, ultimately, assist in the toppling of the Sandinista regime.

If one assumes with NSAs that the Sandinistas are determined to become another Cuba and can be deterred from this course only by persuasion of force, the buildup in Honduras makes a great deal of sense. U.S. Under Secretary of Defense for Policy Fred C. Iklé stated in September 1983 that the consolidation of the Sandinista regime in Nicaragua would necessitate the "partition" of Central America and that the United States would have to "man a new military front line of the East-West conflict, right here on our continent." By this he meant that a hostile Nicaragua, aligned with the Soviet Union, would require the permanent stationing of U.S. troops, as in South Korea and West Germany, in countries bordering Nicaragua to prevent the Sandinistas from sweeping throughout the isthmus. If the Sandinistas have such intentions and administration policy or lack of congressional support for administration policy, does not deter them from this goal, the military buildup in Honduras will be seen as prescient. Meanwhile, argue NSAs, the massive presence of U.S. forces keeps pressure on the Sandinistas, prevents Nicaragua from crossing into Honduras to wipe out the headquarters of the FDN, the largest branch of the *contras*, and ties down substantial numbers of Nicaraguan forces that might otherwise be used to attack the guerrillas on Nicaragua's southern border or in overseas adventures such as those of Cuba.

HRAs are in general less persuaded than NSAs of Nicaragua's aggressive intentions but also are convinced that the buildup and a policy of military pressure may hasten rather than discourage hostile behavior by the Sandinistas. (See "Nicaragua" section in this chapter.)

They are worried about the impact of the buildup in several other areas. One is the way in which the buildup reinforces stereotypes about the United States as an "imperial" power and recalls the bygone era of "gunboat diplomacy" when the United States dictated terms to many Central American countries. They also believe that the strong military stance adopted by the United States undermines rather than supports the Contadora process which seeks negotiated solutions to the region's conflicts.

While the heavy U.S. presence undoubtedly serves as a tripwire to warn the Sandinistas that any incursion into Honduras would produce a response by the United States, HRAs worry that it also exposes the United States to being inadvertently drawn into hostilities. Reconnaissance flights, routine helicopter trips near the border, and the support of private U.S. citizens for the *contras* all have the potential to produce accidental injury or death that could escalate out of control.

Great debate exists as well over the impact of the buildup on U.S.-Honduran relations. NSAs argue that the only thing that could damage U.S.-Honduran relations is if the United States fails to support Honduras strongly enough. In this view, the Hondurans are in favor of progressively closer ties with the United States to protect them from a better-armed and ideologically incompatible Nicaragua. If the United States maintains itself as a firm and resolute ally, no problems will arise between the two countries.

HRAs counter that this perspective on Honduras was given a jolt in 1984 when the head of the Honduran armed forces, General Gustavo

Alvarez Martínez, was ousted by his fellow military officers. A *líder máximo* (maximum leader) in the classic Latin American style, Alvarez had alienated his fellow officers by his arrogant disregard for collegial decision making within the armed forces *and* for being identified too closely with U.S. interests. His replacement, General Walter López, while still friendly to the United States, has made it clear that friendship has a higher price than the one exacted by General Alvarez. On the issues of tacit Honduran support for the *contras*, the training of Salvadorans in the regional military training center in Honduras, and the renegotiation of security and economic relations between the United States and Honduras, General López has been a much tougher bargainer. HRAs point to these developments as early warning signs that the increased U.S. presence in Honduras, while convenient in the short run, could set off forces in the longer term that would ultimately weaken Honduras and the good relations that Honduras and the United States currently enjoy.

A final concern of HRAs about the U.S. buildup in Honduras is the manipulation and perhaps deception of Congress involved in carrying out the policy. As noted in a Congressional Research Service study, critics have charged that "the Administration has violated or ignored congressional mandates, procedures, and prerogatives concerning overseas military construction and the deployment of forces in or near conflict zones." ["Honduras: U.S. Military Activities," by Janice R. Hanover (*Congressional Research Services Review*, January 1985), pp. 14-15.] This debate touches on the sensitive issue, especially controversial since Vietnam, of whether the executive branch has appropriated to itself war-making powers constitutionally reserved to Congress. Since the passage of the War Powers Resolution toward the end of the Vietnam War, the Congress has tried to reassert its prerogative to approve in advance any actions that could involve U.S. forces in hostile actions. For HRAs, the buildup, construction activities, and massive maneuvers have violated the spirit and perhaps the letter of the law. In their analysis, the buildup in Honduras may be the most damaging to the United States because of the way it exacerbates this constitutional dispute.

Question: Does the U.S. Buildup in Honduras Serve Honduran Interests?

Discussion: Some Hondurans would consider this question an example of the arrogance of U.S. attitudes toward Latin America that is at the heart of U.S.-Latin American problems. If the Honduran people through their elected government desire closer ties with the United States and encourage a large U.S. presence in their country, why should the United States preoccupy itself with whether this is really in the interest of Honduras?

The answer for HRAs goes to the admitted fragility of Honduran democracy and the effects on its new democratic practices of a heavy U.S. presence. As we saw in the Honduran "snapshot" in Chapter 2, Honduras has only recently broken a tradition of rule by military strongmen by electing civilian governments in 1981 and 1985. While an encouraging sign, these recent steps are far from making Honduras into a bastion of democracy.

With a largely uneducated and unintegrated rural population, Honduran democracy is so far largely a game for urban elites. The military remains a powerful force behind the throne and has made several public displays of its independence from civilian rule, the most egregious example being General López's announcement of the renegotiation of a U.S.-Honduran security treaty in 1983 without apparent consultation with President Suazo Córdova.

When asked if Hondurans were not pleased by the massive U.S. presence, a Honduran lawyer and social commentator once remarked to an HRA, "Absolutely—especially the prostitutes." What he was implying is that despite payoffs to Honduras, the U.S. buildup has certain inevitable and probably unavoidable corrupting influences on Honduran life.

One is the elevation of the U.S. ambassador to the "proconsul" role that characterized all-powerful U.S. ambassadors in the region fifty years ago. In the first decades of the twentieth century, the U.S. ambassador in Caribbean and Central American countries was the second most powerful person in the country—or at times the most powerful. Presidents and dictators consulted the U.S. ambassador about the details of domestic political life, and military generals tested the reactions of their colleagues at the U.S. embassy before mounting any coups.

The buildup in Honduras and the organizing of the *contra* activities based in Honduras have now placed the U.S. ambassador in this "proconsul" role again. Anti-American sentiment is very low in Honduras but growing. The prominent position of the U.S. ambassador lends credence to those opposed to the current government and to charges that Honduran independence and autonomy are being trampled by the heavy U.S. presence.

Another consequence for Honduras of the buildup is the increased importance given to the military. The Honduran military is now the power behind the throne of a fragile Honduran democracy. While supportive of civilian rule thus far, the military retains a veto over future political developments. The intended impact of the U.S. buildup on Honduran forces is, NSAs argue, to expand, upgrade, and professionalize them. Professionalization means in U.S. terms that they would become an effective but apolitical force concerned with the country's national security and uninvolved in politics.

While this may be the intention of U.S. policy, the historical record of similar efforts causes HRAs to be concerned about the ultimate impact on the Honduran political system of a more confident, better trained and armed, and larger military force. In El Salvador, the closest and most recent example, U.S. aid to the military does seem to have helped control some of its repressive instincts. The knowledge that U.S. congressional support for El Salvador is contingent on democratic practices and acceptance of the reforms advocated by President Duarte seems to have encouraged the military to support elected government and a process of social reform.

In the 1960s and 1970s, however, U.S. training of Latin American military forces had no discernable effect on reinforcing civilian rule and democratic practices. Indeed, some HRAs argue that the military governments that swept to power in Brazil, Argentina, Chile, Uruguay, and other countries were encouraged to think they could do better than civilian politicians by the training and professionalization they had received from the United States and from their own military schools.

HRAs think that any analyst of Latin American affairs would have to be concerned about a policy in Honduras that emphasizes the military dimension as much as current policy does. Many Hondurans already complain that, despite massive U.S. economic and military aid ($230 million in 1984), the military is consuming larger and larger portions of the meager budget available to the government of a poor country such as Honduras. The U.S. buildup is, according to HRAs, at least distorting Honduras' spending priorities and perhaps subtly undermining its infant democratic system.

HRAs feel that anyone familiar with U.S.-Latin American relations would have to wonder, finally, about the long-run impact on Honduras of the massive U.S. presence. In some ways, Honduras was one of the sleepier Central American countries, less polarized by the divisive forces that threatened to tear apart neighbors such as El Salvador and Guatemala and that produced revolution in Nicaragua. HRAs believe that the U.S. presence could accelerate a radicalization of Honduran politics rather than reinforce democracy.

HRAs observe that many of the countries that have had political upheavals threatening to the United States were ones that earlier in the twentieth century had experienced intense relations with, and at times occupations by, the United States (Cuba, the Dominican Republic, Nicaragua, Mexico). NSAs counter that it would be incorrect to draw any direct causal links between the earlier experience of U.S. dominance and later turmoil or to argue that every incidence of heavy involvement by the United States leads to revolutions aimed against the United States.

However, HRAs argue that it is easy for an overwhelming presence by the United States in a Latin American country to create a convenient scapegoat for the opposition and perhaps help to radicalize that opposition. Those supported by the United States, because of the compromises they must inevitably make to gain U.S. favor, are often portrayed by their opposition as *vendepatrias*, sellouts, who surrender national interests for the rewards that a great power can bestow. Opposition figures, who under other circumstances might have to promote their cause on the merits of alternative policies, can take the easier demagogic road of condemning U.S. imperalism as the source of all their country's problems.

Many Americans, raised on images of U.S. troops being received as liberators by grateful Europeans in two world wars, have a hard time understanding the intense hostility displayed toward the United States in many Third World countries. The explanation for this hostility, according to HRAs, is that in the Third World the United States often intervenes not to save a whole people from a foreign invader but to support one political faction against another. Factions seeking United States help have learned to present their case as a struggle to protect their nation against the threat of communism. This kind of intervention is welcomed by some but condemned by others who are defeated because of U.S. support for their adversaries.

Thus, HRAs argue, U.S. policy makers need to be concerned about the long-term effects of the U.S. buildup on Honduras' domestic political cal process and on relations with the United States. Many Hondurans, including the prostitutes, may be pleased with the heavy U.S. presence. But the buildup has certain inevitable side effects that may not be in the best long-term interests of either the United States or of Honduras. As is the case with the next country to be discussed, Costa Rica, HRAs worry that U.S. policy in Honduras runs the risk of sacrificing the long-term stability of Honduras to short-run strategic gains represented by the military buildup.

If pressed, NSAs might have to concede some truth, at least in the abstract, to each of these concerns of HRAs. But they would argue that, while different policies would be desirable in a more perfect world, the United States has to deal with the harsh realities of an increasingly well-armed and hostile Nicaragua sitting on Honduras' border. In the view of NSAs, the only way to deter the Sandinistas from aggression against their neighbors is to maintain the pressure on them that the *contras* provide. To support the *contras*, reassure Honduras and the other Central American countries that the United States will not abandon them to the Marxists, and to be prepared to contain Nicaragua if current policies do not succeed, the United States must play a large role in Honduras. The consequences for Honduras and for the rest of Central America of a diminished U.S. presence would be worse than anything happening now, argue NSAs, if the Sandinistas are allowed to consolidate themselves in power and to act with a free hand in the region.

COSTA RICA

Question: What is the Best Way for Costa Rica to Protect Itself from a Potentially Hostile Nicaragua and Preserve Its Unique Democratic System: Neutrality, or Alliance with the United States?

Discussion: Costa Rica is different from the rest of Central America in many ways. Literate, healthy, moderate in lifestyle as well as politics, Costa Rica is a breath of cool air to the visitor suffocating from travels to the "hot spots" of Central America. Yet Costa Rica in the mid-1980s is beginning to feel the pressures and the polarization of the conflicts raging all around it. Its population is becoming increasingly concerned about the course of the Sandinista revolution in bordering Nicaragua and divided over the best response to it.

As we saw in Chapter 2, Costa Rica has been historically isolated from many events shaping the rest of Central America. Undoubtedly, that is a tradition that many Costa Ricans would like to continue. The government of President Luis Alberto Monge (1982-1986), responding to this sentiment, proclaimed Costa Rica's "perpetual, active and unarmed neutrality" on November 17, 1983. Staying neutral while the rest of Central America flies apart at the seams has not been easy, however. The opposition to the Monge government, Costa Rica's free but conservative press, and some insistent NSA voices in the United States argue that neutrality is an exercise in self-deception when a struggle between democracy and communism is being waged on their doorstep. They fear that with only a poorly equipped Rural and Civil Guard, Costa Rica will not be able to defend itself from an aggressive Sandinista state that desires to "export revolution" in order to maintain its own security. Even if Nicaragua does not threaten Costa Rica directly, they say, it may take advantage of the country's severe economic crisis to sow subversion. Costa Rican conservatives view the Sandinistas as Marxist-Leninists who can never be trusted to abide by agreements. They oppose all talks, negotiations, or agreements between Nicaragua and the United States and are convinced that only the unseating of the

Sandinistas will restore peace in the region. They want to align Costa Rica with a U.S. policy of pressure on the Sandinistas and to increase Costa Rica's military preparedness to resist them.

Those favoring the policy of neutrality also expect to have problems with Nicaragua in the future. But they contend that too close an alliance with the United States can only encourage the Sandinistas to take reprisals against Costa Rica as hostility mounts between the U.S. and Nicaragua. Training a few more guardsmen will not equip Costa Rica to do battle with the vastly superior Nicaraguan armed forces. It will, however, signal Costa Rica's alignment with a policy of confrontation. For many in Costa Rica, Honduras is a telling example of a country that has prostituted itself to U.S. interests, surrendering substantial sovereignty while receiving few benefits.

HRAs point out that Costa Ricans in general have a very benevolent view of the United States. They never suffered occupation or invasion by the "colossus of the North." There is little appreciation among the general public of the potential divergence between Costa Rica's interests as a tiny outpost of democracy and the global concerns of a superpower. Most would find it hard to believe that the United States would use up a country and throw it away when the costs became too high and political support withered at home, although this is what happened to another neutral country surrounded by conflict, Cambodia.

Question: How Can the United States Best Reinforce Costa Rica's Democratic Traditions?

Discussion: As Costa Ricans debate among themselves the best direction for their country, NSAs urge the United States to press for a closer alliance between Costa Rica and the United States. From the NSAs' perspective, Costa Rica needs to get its house in order if it is to resist the aggression being waged by communist forces throughout the region. Part of getting its house in order will be to give its economic policies a more free-market orientation and to join with the other U.S. allies, El Salvador and Honduras, in presenting a united front to the Marxist-Leninists in Nicaragua.

There is no question that Costa Rica's democratic traditions are threatened by its desperate economic conditions. The revolution of 1948 that began the country's democratic tradition also created one of the first "welfare states" in the Western Hemisphere. While coffee prices were good and the economy prospered, Costa Rica could afford to provide reasonably well for its citizens, giving many, especially the middle class, a stake in the democratic system. The economic reversals of the 1970s that affected most of the Third World struck Costa Rica particularly hard. But instead of cutting back on its welfare policies,

Costa Rica borrowed heavily hoping for a future upturn in the economy that never came. Costa Rica in the mid-1980s is in desperate financial straits and has the dubious distinction of having the highest per-capita debt in Latin America.

Since 1983, the United States has been providing steady increases of economic aid to Costa Rica—some $27.2 million in 1983; $152.6 million in 1984; $173.7 million in 1985. As is standard practice, the United States has required changes in Costa Rican economic policies that it views as necessary to assure better performance in the future. These recommendations call for a reduction of the government's role in the economy and an increased emphasis on private-sector initiatives. One particularly sensitive issue has been a call by the United States for the denationalization of Costa Rica's banking system. As a key aspect of the 1948 program of reform, maintaining the banking system in public hands has been a great political importance to the Costa Ricans and is one recommendation they have so far ignored.

The Costa Ricans find themselves in the very difficult position that was faced by another small welfare state in Latin America, Uruguay. Like Costa Rica, Uruguay experienced a middle-class revolution that created an advanced social welfare state, but early in the twentieth century. Financed by grain and beef production, Uruguay's social programs were the basis of a consensual democratic system that lasted until the 1970s. The progressive erosion of Uruguay's economy, however, undermined stability and promoted urban guerrilla warfare that, in turn, produced the classic repressive military reaction. Uruguay returned to democratic practice in 1985 after twelve years of a brutal military dictatorship.

Like Uruguay, Costa Rica can no longer afford the welfare state that has underwritten democratic politics for the last four decades. It must discover new sources of wealth or reach a new consensus about how to distribute wealth within the society. Neither of these alternatives will be easy in the midst of a regional war, domestic polarization, and economic crisis.

NSAs urge the United States to help this process by providing economic assistance to ease the transition. The United States should make clear to Costa Rica that the aid is to support a period of reexamination and the making of hard choices, not a way to avoid decisions that may have high political costs.

HRAs fear that in the midst of what the United States perceives as a grave threat to its security from communism, NSAs will place more emphasis on gaining Costa Rica's support for its regional objectives than on encouraging dialogue among Costa Ricans as to the best course for their country, economically and politically. The United States, HRAs argue, will have to resist the temptation to equate the interests of a small, fragile democracy with its own interests as a superpower in preserving U.S. prerogatives in the region. This will be a tremendous challenge for the United States— one that it has not often met before in its relations with small powers.

GUATEMALA

Question: Does Guatemala's Ruthless and Apparently Successful Elimination of Its Guerrilla Threat Provide Lessons for Other Central American Countries?

Discussion: Due to the unwillingness of its military government to comply with President Carter's human-rights requirements, Guatemala did not receive U.S. assistance for or oversight of its armed forces in the late 1970s. Training and equipment were available from other countries without restrictions but on a reduced basis. By all accounts, the lack of aid and supervision created a do-or-die situation that forced the Guatemalan armed forces back on their own resources. Without the mobility provided by imported helicopters, the army relied on decentralized command structures and extensive patrolling of guerrilla-held territory that put the armed forces into direct contact with the local population. The armed forces resolved to dry up the "sea" of largely Indian peasants in which the guerrillas swam (the classic analogy between guerrillas and peasants and fish in the sea comes from one of the most successful practitioners of guerrilla warfare, Mao Zedung) and adopted a series of measures to accomplish this. These included "civic action" programs that provided work and food for peasants in return for their recruitment into civil self-defense patrols (the so-called *frijoles y fusiles* or "beans and bullets" program). Nominally, every peasant male between the ages of 18 and 60 was required to join his local patrol. The patrols were to monitor suspicious activities in their villages, patrol local roads and paths, and participate in army-led sweeps of the area and in training exercises. "Model villages" were created into which thousands of peasants were moved so that they could be watched by the army and prevented from becoming a support base for the guerrillas.

Between 1980 and 1982, the army waged a brutal war in the countryside, killing thousands of peasants and community leaders who were suspected (or merely accused) of sympathizing with the guerrillas. The coup of March 1982, which brought the fanatical General Efraín Ríos Montt to power, resulted in a decline in political murders and kidnappings in some areas. The civil-defense strategy already described was adopted and the rural environment stabilized to some degree. Ríos Montt's inefficient and erratic governing style, enforced with a born-again Christianity in a predominantly Catholic country, resulted in his replacement by Brigadier General Oscar Mejía Victores in 1983. The strategy for conducting the war continued largely unchanged.

Judged on its own terms, Guatemala's counterinsurgency war was very successful. Guatemala City and much of the rural countryside is now pacified. As recently as 1982, the capital was like an armed camp, periodically racked by terrorist explosions. Within miles of the city, guerrillas controlled large areas of the country, stopping cars, issuing travel passes, and collecting revolutionary taxes. Reports in 1985 indicated that the guerrillas, once 4,000 strong, had been reduced to 2,500 and were concentrated in the border provinces near Mexico. The lessened security risk and a renewed concern for Guatemala's international image led in 1984 and 1985 to relative reductions in political killings and "disappearances" (from a high of about 500 political murders a month, mostly by the right, to about 100 a month in 1984-1985) and to elections resulting in civilian rule.

As Guatemala has stabilized and begun to inch toward civilian rule, the United States has indicated its readiness to resume military and economic aid to the country. The leaders of Guatemala's 30,000-strong army disdain advice from a country that lost its first sustained guerrilla war in Vietnam and is restrained by public opinion from waging Guatemala-style warfare. But the army's civic action programs and "model villages" require economic assistance that the declining Guatemalan economy cannot provide.

Now that the dirty work is done, NSAs argue that the United States can renew assistance without compromising itself too badly. HRAs are troubled by the nagging question of whether "victory" Guatemala-style will become the model for U.S. policy elsewhere in the region where military defeat of guerrillas is the ultimate objective.

QUESTION: Will U.S. Military and Economic Assistance Strengthen the Apparent Democratic Opening in Guatemala or Will It Encourage a Mere Democratic Facade?

DISCUSSION: The series of political murders of prominent human-rights activists that struck Guatemala in the spring of 1985 produced a necessary realism about the prospects for an easy return to civilian democratic rule in Guatemala—something that has not existed since 1954. But several positive developments in 1984 and 1985 also surprised many outside observers.

General Mejía has promoted some liberalization in Guatemala. Most significant was his decision to support elections for a legislative assembly in July 1984. After years of brutal repression in which everyone to the left of the army—teachers, students, union leaders, human rights activists, moderate politicians—had seemingly been killed, "disappeared," or been intimidated, most observers expected a tainted election with a right-wing outcome. Instead, a moderate center emerged with the majority of the popular vote. Complicated proportional representation schemes led the traditional extreme right-wing party to receive more seats in the Constituent Assembly than their popular vote would have suggested. But the balance of power in the assembly, which called presidential elections for November 1985 and drafted a new constitution, lay with center and liberal parties.

In the runoff presidential elections of December 1985, moderate Christian Democrat Marco Vinicio Cerezo Arévalo emerged the victor. A dedicated democrat who had been the object of assassination attempts by a previous military government, Vinicio Cerezo began the first civilian government in 15 years with modest expectations. He argued that his government must try to stop future human rights violations, but that past deaths and disappearances could not be investigated because the military would impose, as he put it, "obvious limits." He added, with impressive candor, that the military had only agreed to give him the office of president. It would require political skill and effort on his part to exercise real power.

Given their desire to renew ties with Guatemala, NSAs emphasize the positive aspects of recent developments. Guatemala is now routinely included in the litany of democracies (El Salvador, Costa Rica, Honduras) said to be developing in the region as a result of U.S. policy and as contrasted with undemocratic Nicaragua. The United States gave $300,000 in military assistance and $75.3 million in economic aid to Guatemala in 1985 and has requested $10.3 million in military aid and $76.9 million in economic aid for 1986. NSAs believe that U.S. aid will reinforce democratic developments in the country and gain some leverage for the United States over Guatemala's stance in the Contadora process, where it has sided more with its neighbor Mexico than with the United States and its allies, Honduras and El Salvador.

HRAs point out that, given their pride in having won a guerilla war without U.S. help and their belief that the human-rights strings attached to U.S. aid could restrain future conduct, Guatemala's military leaders are not overly eager to embrace the U.S. offer of assistance. They need aid to finance their "model village" program but will resist strictures on their prosecution of the counterinsurgency campaign or pressures to support U.S. positions in Contadora that they feel are insulting to national dignity and independence. Newly elected civilian president Vinicio Cerezo gave early signs of his desire to avoid too close an alliance with U.S. hostility toward Nicaragua by visiting Sandinista president Daniel Ortega in his preinaugural tour of all the Central American countries; a visit that reportedly angered U.S. officials.

Even after the best of all possible transitions to democracy, the Guatemalan army will remain, like its counterpart in Honduras, the power behind the civilian throne. HRAs emphasize this fact when insisting that the United States distance itself from a system that has been among the cruelest in Central America. In their view, recent developments in Guatemala are more appearance than reality. To renew U.S. aid at this time would be to signal the generals that a democratic facade is all that is needed to please external opinion while allowing the military to solidify its hold over the country without promoting basic political and economic reforms.

In the flawed and morally ambiguous world in which the NSA believes the United States must operate, the relatively positive developments in Guatemala provide the opportunity for the United States to regain influence with a strategic regional actor. This influence can be used to reinforce democratic developments in the country and to coordinate Guatemala's positions in Contadora more closely with those of the United States.

AM I AN NSA OR AN HRA?

If you are feeling frustrated by this back-and-forth debate between NSAs and HRAs, you are not alone. The exchange of views about Central America taking place in Washington is not always illuminating. It reflects personal prejudices, disagreements about some of the basic facts, and, as we have tried to show, different views about how the United States should conduct its foreign policy in the world in which it finds itself.

Many books on Central America want to persuade you of the wisdom of a particular solution to the conflict. Our goal is different. We hope to encourage you to think through your own position while providing some signposts that lead you from one issue to another. The NSA/HRA checklist that follows is an attempt to summarize basic differences in the approaches of NSAs and HRAs. You will probably not find yourself in complete agreement with either of the thumbnail sketches of our two stereotypes. But before you leave this chapter, see if you can find the logic, or lack of it, in each stereotype or in some new set of assumptions and policy prescriptions that you can devise.

HOW DO I KNOW IF I'M A NATIONAL SECURITY ANALYST (NSA) OR A HUMAN RIGHTS ACTIVIST (HRA)?

NSA Checklist

1. The United States, although it may have its flaws, is the greatest defender of freedom and democracy in the world today.————

2. The world would be a much better place if more countries adopted the values and practices of the United States, and it should be a goal of U.S. policy to see that that happens.————

3. Unfortunately, the United States exists in a world in which many nation-states do not share its goals and use every means to thwart the objectives of U.S. policy.————

4. As long as such a situation exists, the United States must use every means available, including some it would otherwise find reprehensible, to defend itself and its allies.————

5. Principal among the threats to the peace and security of the United States is communism, especially as it is embodied and practiced by the Soviet Union.————

6. It must be a central goal of U.S. foreign policy to prevent the creation of any new communist regimes in the world, particularly in a region close to the United States such as Central America.————

7. The Soviet Union, directly or through its ally Cuba, is behind many of the problems in Central America and would be the prime beneficiary if current U.S. policy in the region does not succeed.————

8. The United States has the power, if only it will use it, to prevent communist victories in Central America.————

9. In the case of El Salvador, the prevention of communist victory means support for the Salvadoran government until the leftist guerrillas recognize the futility of their insurgency and return to the democratic process or are defeated militarily.————

10. In the case of Nicaragua, the prevention of communist victory means persuading the Sandinista government, by force if necessary, to abandon its totalitarian designs for Nicaragua and to accept a democratic government elected by free and fair elections.————

11. In both El Salvador and Nicaragua, these defeats for communism can be achieved without the direct use of U.S. military force and/or troops. But the success of this policy is so important for U.S. interests that the United States must remain prepared to use direct force and/or troops if necessary. Eliminating this option for the United States would only encourage forces hostile to our interests.————

12. In Honduras, Costa Rica, and Guatemala, the United States must pursue policies that support its goals for El Salvador and Nicaragua while encouraging stability and democratic government in the three countries.———

HRA Checklist

1. The United States has an enviable, though imperfect, record of honoring human rights within its own borders.———

2. The world would be a much better place if more countries adopted the human rights practices of the United States, and it should be a goal of U.S. policy to see that that happens.———

3. Unfortunately, a majority of governments around the world, especially in the Third World and in the socialist bloc, engage in systematic violations of human rights.———

4. In response to these violations, the United States should adopt a foreign policy designed to promote a climate of human-rights protection, based on respect for persons and the principle of law.———

5. Under no circumstances should the United States support governments that systematically violate human rights. In the long run, principled behavior based on human rights as the cornerstone of U.S. foreign policy will do the most to protect U.S. national security by encouraging more equitable, responsive governments and hence a more peaceful world.———

6. The underlying cause of unrest in Central America is the social injustice created by centuries of repression and exploitation.———

7. The Soviet Union and Cuba may seek to take advantage of this unrest for their own purposes, but cannot ultimately succeed if more just governments, respectful of human rights, are supported in the region.———

8. The United States does not have the right and lacks the resources to prevent the development of socialist governments in Central America unless those governments directly threaten the security of the United States by installing Soviet or Cuban bases or strategic weapons that are capable of attacking the United States.———

9. In the case of El Salvador, the United States can best promote human rights and a more just government by seeking a political, negotiated solution to the Salvadoran civil war.———

10. In the case of Nicaragua, the United States can best promote human rights and a more just government by pressuring the Sandinista government through peaceful means and diplomatic negotiations. No invasion of Nicaragua is justified unless the Sandinistas install strategic weapons or bases or directly attack their neighbors.———

11. Direct U.S. military force or troops should not be introduced into Central America.———

12. The pursuit of peaceful, political, and diplomatic solutions to the conflicts in El Salvador and Nicaragua has the best chance to promote democratic government in Costa Rica, Honduras, and Guatemala.————

NOTES

1. These publications are available to the public from S/LPD Room 5917, U.S. Department of State, Washington, DC 20530. *Background Paper: Nicaragua's Military Build-up and Support for Central American Subversion* (July 1984); *Comandante Bayardo Arce's Secret Speech before the Nicaraguan Socialist Party* (1984); *Broken Promises: Sandinista Repression of Human Rights in Nicaragua* (October 1984); *Resource Book: Sandinista Elections in Nicaragua* (Fall 1984); *Misconceptions About U.S. Policy Toward Nicaragua* (two issues: September 1984 and March 1985); *The Soviet-Cuban Connection in Central America and the Caribbean* (March 1985); *The Sandinista Military Build-up* (May 1985—an update of *Background Paper*); *The Sandinistas and Middle Eastern Radicals* (August 1985).

2. Nicaraguan president Daniel Ortega, in an October 2, 1985, speech before the United Nations said, "If peace does not come and war continues, and with it the possibility of a North American intervention, the whole world should know that the Nicaraguan people, barefoot, in rags, and hungry, will fight to the end, until we achieve peace by defeating the invader, or until we immolate ourselves, if imperalist aggression requires we do so."

3. There is no official definition of what military victory in El Salvador means. When asked, most administration spokespersons respond that it entails the reduction over five years or so of the Salvadoran guerrillas to a small group of bandits operating at relatively low levels in approximately 10 percent of the national territory.

Making Your Voice Heard:
How To Influence Central American Policy

This book has a hidden agenda: to persuade you that what the United States is doing in Central America should be of concern to you and that you should involve yourself in the policy debate about the region. We have tried to tell the story of Central America in the fairest way we know how. As professionals who spend a great deal of time focused on Central America we obviously have our own individual policy preferences. But we believe that our pet policies to resolve all the problems of Central America are less important than the involvement of greater numbers of citizens in the debate over an issue that could affect your own life and already influences the lives of millions of Central Americans.

A grasp of the basic history of the region and an understanding of the policy debate as it occurs in Washington are essential prerequisites for playing a meaningful role in the policy process. But you also need to know that individual citizens, by combining their energies with those of other individuals, have changed the course of U.S. policy toward Central America. Whether you're an NSA in substantial agreement with current policy or an HRA troubled by many aspects of U.S. relations with the region, there are ways to make your voice heard inside the Beltway. The first step is to identify, as best you can, where you stand in the policy debate. Our checklist of HRA "traits" and NSA "traits" at the end of Chapter 3 should have been a useful beginning.

INFLUENCING WASHINGTON

Once you have decided whether you are an NSA or an HRA or wish to pursue some set of policy preferences different from either of our

"...I wonder what would happen if I went crazy and stood up."

"*Indigenous reform, even indigenous revolution, is not a security threat to the United States.*"

—Kissinger Commission Report, 1984

"*Despite the Commission's claims to the contrary, the position it lays out places the United States in opposition to* any *revolutionary change in Central America.*"

—William M. LeoGrande, "Through the Looking Glass: The Kissinger Report on Central America," *World Policy Journal*, winter 1984

stereotypes, it is time to focus on the policy process in Washington and how you can influence it. You have basically three strategies for doing so: the insider strategy, the outsider strategy and the radical-outsider strategy. Each is explained below.

Insider Strategy. The most obvious way to affect policy toward Central America is to become a policy maker yourself. This may sound like a drastic step. But it is in fact the way that many of those inside the

Beltway first began their careers in public service: they were attracted to or repelled by what was happening in Washington and determined to do something about it. You can probably come up with examples yourself if you stop to think for a moment. The young idealists who were attracted by the forceful personality of Franklin Roosevelt and his "New Deal" for the United States, the generations who came to work on the "New Frontier" of John F. Kennedy or the "New American Revolution" of Ronald Reagan are also examples. There are now a number of Vietnam veterans in Congress. They share the experience of having participated in that war but often have very different prescriptions, both liberal and conservative, about how to prevent future Vietnams.

Beyond elective office, one can work for the executive branch of government in the White House, State Department, Defense Department, or other agencies, or in the legislative branch as a member of a congressman's personal staff or on the numerous committee staffs. Some who come to Washington choose to work on the fringes of policy making in "think tanks," research centers, lobbying organizations, and other institutions that seek to affect the outcome of policy debates without having the ability to directly make policy themselves. Each of these insider jobs has the advantage of dealing with policy more or less directly. Each also has the disadvantage of forcing one to adopt the Washington mentality of focusing on the practical, the do-able, and the politically acceptable.

Outsider Strategy. If you don't want to or can't come to Washington to become a policy maker yourself you can still seek to influence policy from outside the Beltway. It might be helpful to you as an outsider to know what the policy-making establishment in Washington thinks about you, the average citizen. Because the United States is a representative democracy, elected officials have to be responsive to voters' opinions if they want to be reelected. But the voting public varies greatly in the amount of attention it gives to policy in general and to foreign policy in particular.

Specialists in the field of public opinion talk about three different types of publics: the mass public, the attentive public, and opinion makers. The mass public, estimated at 75 percent of the population, is said to be generally uninterested and uninformed about foreign-policy issues unless their own lives are directly affected by something happening overseas (as in the case of Vietnam, where losing a son in the war often motivated parents to become more politically aware). The second public is the attentive public, that 10 percent of the population that remains active and well-informed on foreign-policy issues. The third public is a small group of opinion makers, who often play leadership roles in their communities and who help to shape the opinions of their fellow citizens.

The attentive public and opinion makers can be local elected officials, religious leaders, journalists, or professors. Many are members of community organizations such as the Jaycees, Women's Club, or Rotary Club, as well as local foreign-policy or world-affairs councils, or religious and ethnic organizations. The interest and influence of these associations varies from issue to issue and from group to group. For example, the religious community and its leaders, conservative and liberal alike, have been the single most active and influential group on Central American issues. They have a broad constituency to represent and use every device possible—lobbying, petitions, media attention, sit-ins—to make their voices heard.

Washington insiders want to hear from you in order to assess the level of public support for their favorite policies or to assure their reelection, but they are also very confused about how seriously to take your opinions. On the issue of Central America, for example, poll after poll shows that citizens have very strong views about the use of U.S. troops anywhere in the region. Big majorities oppose an invasion of Nicaragua. But only about 25 percent of those responding to these polls can correctly identify which side the United States supports in El Salvador and Nicaragua. Strongly held views based on relative ignorance do not inspire confidence among political leaders in the opinions of the mass public or make for good democratic practices.

If you are an outsider you should also know something about the foreign-policy-making process. In the case of Central America, as on many other foreign-policy issues, the key dilemma is the conflict between the executive branch (the president, his cabinet, the departments, and agencies) and the legislative branch (the Congress, and its staff and committees). In their wisdom the founding fathers charged the president with primary responsibility for making and carrying out foreign policy. When Congress agrees on a bipartisan basis with the direction of foreign policy, as it did for much of the post-Second World War period, things run more or less smoothly. When Congress disagrees or when a bipartisan consensus breaks down, as it has since the Vietnam War, foreign policy becomes a political battleground. Congress may not be able constitutionally to make foreign policy, but it can be rather effective at unmaking foreign policy by harassing the executive branch with resolutions, legislative restrictions, guidelines, hearings, the denial of presidential appointments, and control of the budget. Having a president from one party in the White House and the control of one or both houses of Congress in the hands of the other party more or less guarantees a confused and confusing foreign policy. If you're an HRA you probably offer thanks each night that Congress has had the sense to restrain the Reagan administration and wish they would be even more aggressive. If you're an NSA you're probably frustrated and angry that what the United States needs to do in Central America is seemingly undermined at every turn by a hostile Congress. This conflict between the legislative and executive branches is a built-in aspect of U.S. democracy that can be overcome only when most citizens agree and can develop a foreign policy on the basis of consensus.

Despite this constitutional conflict, it is the president and the executive branch that retain the first, and often the final, say in foreign policy. Depending on the president and the issue, advice is sought from the heads of agencies involved in foreign policy—some fifty in number, ranging from the Environmental Protection Agency to the Department of Commerce—and from a foreign-policy inner circle. The inner circle includes the secretary of state, secretary of defense, director of the Central Intelligence Agency, chairman of the Joint Chiefs of Staff, National Security Council adviser, and personal political advisers attuned to the president's agenda and the possible effects of policy on his popularity. Individual members of Congress, as opposed to Congress as an institution, may be brought into the inner circle on occasion because of their expertise or chairmanship of key committees. Select members of the Senate Foreign Relations Committee, the House Foreign Affairs Committee, and the Appropriations, Intelligence, and Armed Services committees often work closely with the State Department and the White House to assure support for important foreign-policy decisions. A recent exception to this general practice proves the rule of executive preeminence in the foreign-policy-making process: before the United States invaded the island of Grenada in 1983, no one outside a few executive-branch officials was consulted. In imposing a trade embargo against Nicaragua, President Reagan was not required to confer with anyone, although he did with members of Congress.

Because U.S. involvement in Central America is now so intense, myriad parts of the government are involved in debates over the making of policy toward the region. The National Security Council staff is charged with coordinating the recommendations that come to the president from all over the government and in trying to ensure that the president's policies are faithfully carried out. This is, to say the least, a very big job. On the NSC staff are analysts who specialize in Latin American issues and who may have particular expertise on Central America. They, reflecting their closeness to the president, generally take a hard line on policy toward Central America and come closest to approximating our NSA stereotype.

The State Department is also an important actor in Central America. Its political, economic, commercial, and consular officers contribute an important part of the information and analysis that flows to Washington about the region. Within the department is a Bureau of

Inter-American Affairs devoted exclusively to U.S.-Latin American relations, headed by an assistant secretary. Below the assistant secretary are deputy assistant secretaries, one of whom is especially charged with supervising Central American issues. He in turn has a director of the Office of Central American and Panamanian Affairs and so on down the line to the individual desk officers who concentrate exclusively on one country. The State Department often labors under the burden of being perceived as "soft" because it specializes in diplomacy and tends to look for political solutions to problems.

The Defense Department is also heavily involved in Central America: U.S. military advisers in three of the countries, maneuvers and training bases in Honduras, surveillance and intelligence activities that are highly secret, etc. Before the recent trouble in Central America, Defense had a very low profile in Latin America outside of the Panama Canal. All that has now changed, and Spanish is one of the most popular languages for officers on the way up. Defense is organized more by function than by region. One of the top officials concerned with Central America is the under secretary for policy. Defense is generally assumed to be hard-line on Central America—worried about the Soviets, favoring military solutions, etc. But the Pentagon is also extremely wary of fighting another war without strong popular support, as occurred in Vietnam, and is concerned about tying down scarce resources in Central America. If massive U.S. military involvement in the region develops, it will probably be ordered by civilians and somewhat reluctantly carried out by the military.

Many Latin Americans think the Central Intelligence Agency lurks behind every bush, but there really is deep involvement of the CIA in Central America. The CIA role in assisting the *contras* is well documented, and there are undoubtedly numerous other activities being conducted by the agency in the areas of intelligence gathering and analysis about which little is supposed to be known. As public constraints on the conduct of foreign policy have increased in recent years, the CIA has often become the agent chosen to carry out policy.

In the Congress, the House Foreign Affairs Committee and especially its Subcommittee on Western Hemisphere Affairs, and the Senate Foreign Relations Committee have important roles in Central American policy by being the focal point for rallying public support against or in favor of a particular administration policy. Your own senators and representative may well be on one of these committees, be interested in Central America, or be willing to become so if enough constituents like you make your views known to them.

Outsiders have several effective strategies for affecting policy. Until you have worked in Washington it's probably hard to believe the power of letters. But they do influence Congressmen, the State Department, and the White House. You can write individual letters or, with greater effect, organize letter-writing campaigns by your school, church, club, or association. Volume is important. But often thousands of mimeoed letters signed without apparent thought or copied from standard forms are less effective than a sincere, heartfelt letter that a staffer brings to a Congressman's attention. Linking up with groups with which you have some association can multiply your impact. Your union, club, church, professional association, chamber of commerce, or other organization may have an office in Washington, send a delegation to Washington (especially effective if they have visited Central America as well), or have another mechanism for letting officials know that their membership of hundreds, thousands, or millions is genuinely concerned about what happens in Central America. The freeing of the Salvadoran union leaders through pressure from U.S. union officials, described in Case Study Three later in this chapter, is an example of such an example of such an "outsider" strategy.

Radical-Outsider Strategy. The radical outsider is distinguished from the outsider by a difference in tactics. The radical outsider is not willing to play by the established rules of the game and seeks to change the context within which policy is debated. The antiwar movement of the 1960s is an example of a radical-outsider strategy that used a variety of tactics, including some that were violent and illegal, to try to change specific policies in the Vietnam War and the style of politics in the United States. Experts will debate whether the protests hastened the end of the war or prolonged it, but the movement had a profound cultural impact and important political repercussions, including its contribution to the neoconservative backlash that brought Ronald Reagan to the White House.

In the case of Central America, a radical-outsider strategy is represented by Civilian Military Assistance, an organization of 2,500 former military personnel based in Decatur, Alabama, that raises funds to buy weapons for the Salvadoran military and the Nicaraguan *contras* and has participated in field operations with both groups. Fiercely anticommunist, Civilian Military Assistance feels that the administration has been too restrained by domestic public opinion and seeks to move U.S. policy more strongly toward direct military support of the anticommunist cause in Central America.

Another example of a radical-outsider strategy is provided by the sanctuary movement described below in Case Study One, which outlines the recourse of church groups to civil disobedience to protest their disagreement with current policy.

By mentioning these radical-outsider strategies we are not, of course, endorsing their activities or recommending illegal measures. Nor would we predict that they are likely to be more successful than the other approaches discussed earlier. But you should be aware that in the annals of political practices, radical-outsider strategies have often been used and, at times, proved effective.

What follows are several case studies of how ordinary and not-so-ordinary citizens became concerned enough about Central America to try to affect the course of policy. Not all attempts succeed; we have focused on efforts that did manage to penetrate the policy apparatus and made Washington move faster or in a slightly different direction than it might have otherwise. If some of what you have read in this book has touched you enough to make you want to affect policy toward Central America, here are some examples of how to make your voice heard in Washington.

CASE STUDY ONE: RADICAL-OUTSIDER STRATEGY

In January 1985, James Corbett, a retired rancher, and John Fife, a minister of the Tucson United Presbyterian Church, were indicted on charges of conspiring to smuggle illegal aliens into the United States. They, along with the fourteen other average citizens indicted with them, are part of a grassroots movement of civil disobedience called the sanctuary movement. Mr. Corbett, 51, founded an "underground railroad" in 1981 in Tucson, Arizona, to bring Central Americans into the United States. Reverend Fife was the first minister in the United States to openly declare his church a sanctuary for Central American refugees in March 1982. In June 1984, a director and a volunteer from a Texas refugee shelter were convicted on similar conspiracy charges.

Sanctuary activists work to help Central Americans—primarily Salvadorans and Guatemalans—cross the border illegally from Mexico and offer the safe haven of the church after their arrival. Later the activists help the refugees settle into their new communities by providing housing, employment, and language classes. These sanctuary workers contend that they are not breaking U.S. law by helping Central Americans slip into the country because both the 1980 Refugee Act and international law grant legal aslyum to those who are fleeing political persecution. The U.S. government argues that the aliens come to the United States for economic reasons and that allegations of widespread persecution against those deported back to their home countries have not been documented.

Only a handful in 1981, sanctuary activists and supporters now work through more than two hundred individual churches and synagogues throughout the United States, centered predominantly in the Southwest, the Middle West, California, New York, and New Jersey.

There is no typical activist in the sanctuary movement; rather their occupations and convictions cut across the political and economic spectrum. Activists come from all major religions and are usually supportive of the movement because of their respect for the Judeo-Christian tradition of providing sanctuary. Often they have become concerned about Central America through a friend or acquaintance who has told them horror stories of poverty and violence. Some activists are very strongly opposed to U.S. policy in Central America and use the sanctuary movement as one means to demonstrate their opposition.

The National Council of Churches, the umbrella group for some thirty-one Protestant denominations, does not advocate breaking the law, yet tacitly supports providing assistance to fleeing Central Americans. In a November 1984 policy statement, the Council asked for a moratorium on the deportation of Central Americans and an end to government harassment and prosecution of sanctuary activists. Petitions have been presented to Congress from high-level representatives of all major religions asking the same. In addition, Senator DeConcini (Democrat-Arizona) and Representative Moakley (Democrat-Massachusetts) have introduced a bill requesting that Salvadorans be given "extended voluntary departure" (EVD) status. If passed, this bill would suspend the detention and deportation of Salvadorans for two years until security and humanitarian problems in El Salvador could be fully studied.

Lesson: The sanctuary movement is a dramatic example of everyday citizens taking policy into their own hands by civil disobedience. As is the case with most strategies of civil disobedience, the sanctuary movement gains part of its power from the moral force of common people standing up to their government over a strongly held principle. Just as the church in Central America provided some protection for political protest, churches in the United States also lend their moral authority to these activists concerned about Central American policy. As radical outsiders, those in the sanctuary movement will not directly change U.S. policy. But they will focus media attention on the plight of Salvadorans in El Salvador and in the United States and raise larger questions about the role of the United States in Central America.

CASE STUDY TWO: INSIDER STRATEGY

In July 1983, second-term representative William McCollum, a Republican from near Orlando, Florida, and a staunch supporter of the Reagan administration's policy in Central America, made what is now the usual three-day foray to El Salvador. Representative

McCollum made the customary rounds, including visits to the camps for displaced persons that are scattered throughout El Salvador. What Representative McCollum saw shocked him. There was complete lack of essential medical supplies and equipment, even such basics as aspirin, gauze, disinfectant, and needles, not only for refugees in the camps and for doctors in clinics, but also for soldiers in the field. Supplies needed to perform the simplest kinds of surgery were unavailable. Some rich Salvadorans flew to Miami to have operations and to stock up on aspirin for their friends, but most Salvadorans simply did without.

Representative McCollum returned to the United States determined to convince his staff, friends, constituents, and political contributors of the need for medicine and equipment of the most basic kinds in El Salvador. There was a tremendous response, and by August 5 the first shipment of 5,000 pounds of donated pharmaceutical and health supplies was flown by two volunteers to El Salvador on a borrowed C-47. Another plane flew down August 15 with 15,000 pounds of donated supplies, and in November another 100,000 pounds was shipped.

Representative McCollum's office secured the donations and worked with Project Hope and the Salvadoran Knights of Malta (an international Catholic relief brotherhood) to coordinate what was needed, how it should be packaged, and how to store and distribute it once it reached El Salvador. After the initial legwork spurred by Representative McCollum, the project snowballed, with pharmaceutical companies donating two medicines for the price of one and a variety of Americans and Salvadorans from all walks of life donating time and energy to the project. Vaughn Forest, who managed the effort with Representative McCollum, found that people of all political persuasions, including guerrilla sympathizers, were involved. Medicine was delivered to 117 towns, 60 clinics, displaced-persons camps in the heart of contested zones, and to soldiers in the field.

For his humanitarian effort, Representative McCollum was named "Man of the Year" in January 1984 by the Salvadoran Chamber of Commerce. His efforts, and those of volunteers in El Salvador and the United States, brought a total of 300,000 pounds of health-care supplies, valued at $4 million, to El Salvador's needy. All but $500,000 came from private donations.

Lesson: The experience of Representative McCollum is an example of an insider's strategy affecting policy. In organizing the relief effort, he had the benefit of being a prominent Florida citizen with extensive contacts on which he could draw. But the relief effort was ultimately successful because of the willingness of private citizens to volunteer time and because of the generosity of companies and others who made humanitarian contributions. As a congressman, Representative

McCollum had the ability to request and receive help from the U.S. Agency for International Development. However, a persistent, concerned citizen could organize a similar effort, draw the local media's attention and elicit the involvement of his or her congressman or senator. If you can't commit that much time to such an effort, a less-overwhelming option is to contribute time, money, or energy to one of the two dozen U.S. private-assistance programs operating in Central America.

CASE STUDY THREE: OUTSIDER STRATEGY

In 1982, eleven members of the Salvadoran Electrical Workers Union (STECEL) were detained, accused of conspiring to blow up electrical grids, and imprisoned. The eleven detainees were never formally charged with a crime, nor prosecuted. This was not unusual in El Salvador, where numerous union leaders have been detained without charges or murdered by right-wing death squads, simply for engaging in legal union activities. While common in El Salvador, this situation was contrary to Salvadoran and international human-rights law.

Major U.S. unions decided to demonstrate solidarity with the difficulties faced by Salvadoran unions by making an all-out effort on behalf of the eleven workers. The national union leadership in the United States began a campaign to educate the district leadership and rank-and-file membership about the case through newsletters and personal pleas. They promoted a letter-writing campaign to the Congress, the U.S. State Department, the U.S. embassy in San Salvador, and the Salvadoran government. Each agency/individual was urged to push for either a trial or freedom for the detainees. Several delegates of U.S. labor leaders made trips to El Salvador to visit the detainees and to make personal pleas to the U.S. ambassador and to the Salvadoran government. In October 1984, Salvadoran president Napoleon Duarte ordered the release of the eleven detainees, who were subsequently offered asylum by the Netherlands government.

Lesson: Focusing public attention on a single issue can be an effective strategy. In this case, the international pressure brought to bear on the STECEL workers' case was part of the reason the U.S. embassy repeatedly expressed its concerns to the Salvadoran government for these particular workers. President Duarte himself felt the effects of the worldwide media attention.

If you become aware of a particular issue or situation in Central America, or of a policy or action by the U.S. government, with which you disagree or which you support, let your congressman, senator, ambassador, the State Department, etc., know with a letter or telegram. Better yet, join or form a group to have a more forceful impact on Washington and on Central America itself. Many professional, church, and community groups have an interest in international affairs and may exert pressure on your behalf if asked to do so. It may be easier, and more effective, for you to tackle one problem at a time, and to concern yourself with similar institutions/individuals in Central America, rather than the whole of Central America. In this case study, the connection between workers in El Salvador and workers in the United States was critical to the effective lobbying that was done. Similarly, journalists, doctors, lawyers, religious workers, teachers, and other professionals have all been actively involved with Central America through their professional associations.

CASE STUDY FOUR: INSIDER-OUTSIDER STRATEGY

Another example of citizen support having an impact on U.S. policy in Central America is the lobbying effort on behalf of aid to the *contras*, or Nicaraguan resistance fighters, that occurred in the spring of 1985. *Contra* funding had been identified as a priority for the administration and was a personal commitment of President Reagan's. Insiders in the White House and the Congress worked closely with outsiders in private conservative associations and think tanks to rally support to the president's cause.

The conservative Citizens for America budgeted $300,000 for a campaign in support of the funding for the Nicaraguan rebels. Among the steps taken by the organization was a national tour for twenty-two Central American business leaders who made media appearances and gave speeches on behalf of the funding. Jack Abramoff, the group's executive director, said the purpose of the nationwide tour was "to take the president's case right to the people, to hop right over the national media and get them [the Central Americans] right to the local areas." After the tour, the group of Central Americans came to Washington to lobby directly with members of Congress opposed to or wavering on aid to the *contras*.

As opponents of the aid had done for their side, supporters of funding brought media personalities and other "stars" to Washington to make an impression on the Congress. A group of Western European politicians and writers, called Resistance International, endorsed U.S.

aid to the *contras* at an April 19 White House meeting. The group included Winston Churchill, a Conservative Party member of the British Parliament and grandson of the late British prime minister.

A loose coalition of groups supporting the president's request called the Central America Action Committee met to coordinate lobbying strategy. Attending the meetings were individuals and organizations identified with conservative causes such as the Council for Inter-American Security; the Council for National Policy; the National Forum Foundation; *Human Events* magazine; and representatives from the Office of Public Diplomacy of the State Department and the Office of Public Liaison from the White House; congressional staffers; and individuals from the Republican party affiliates. Some of these groups were involved in organizing letter-writing campaigns and creating and funding radio advertisements in support of the proposed aid.

The initial vote on the *contra* funding in April 1985 was a defeat for the president when the House failed to approve even humanitarian assistance. The defeat came in part because of the massive lobbying by groups opposed to the funding. But Nicaraguan president Ortega's trip to Moscow to request additional military assistance from the Soviet Union, immediately after the *contra* vote, changed the climate of opinion in Washington. In June, Congress voted humanitarian assistance at double the level originally proposed by the president in April.

In addition, grassroots organizations located outside Washington have taken various steps in favor of the *contras*. These individuals also make their voices heard in Washington. Examples of these pro-*contra* groups are the Houston-based Nicaraguan Patriotic Society, which offers a speaker's bureau; the Civilian Military Assistance group; the World Anti-Communist League, which claims to raise as much as $500,000 per month from individual and corporate *contra*-supporters; and the New Orleans-based Caribbean Commission, which has a sponsorship program called "Adopt-a-*Contra*."

Lesson: Because there is a sympathetic audience in the White House, outsiders concerned about Central America who consider themselves NSAs or support measures in Central America stronger than those being pursued by the administration often find their efforts linked up with White House strategy. This has its obvious advantages of power and influence. It may also have the disadvantage of making powerful insiders less concerned about cultivating grassroots support for their policies. If you are in general agreement with administration policy, don't take it for granted that your interests are being defended by those in Washington. They may be as anxious as the rest of Washington to know what "the people back home" are really thinking.

CASE STUDY FIVE: OUTSIDER STRATEGY

On the evening of December 2, 1980, four American churchwomen who had been working with poor and displaced persons in El Salvador were kidnapped, sexually assaulted, and murdered by five National Guardsmen. The brutal murder, and subsequent painfully slow process of justice for their murderers, made the violence and brutality of Central America real for many North Americans for the first time. One congressional staffer for a representative from the home district of two of the women described the churchwomen's case as "the match that lit the flame for a great deal of self-education and awareness on the Central American issue."

On the day of the murder, two of the women, Ursline sister Dorothy Kazel and lay worker Jean Donovan, had driven out to the international airport to meet two colleagues, Maryknoll sisters Ita Ford and Maura Clarke. Unknown to them, a National Guardsman at the airport, who thought they looked suspicious, notified his commander. The commander, a subsergeant, ordered five guardsmen to change into civilian clothes, gather their weapons, and accompany him on an unspecified mission. They waited at the checkpoint close to the airport, apprehended the women, and drove them to an isolated spot where they sexually assaulted and, on the command of the subsergeant, shot them. After burning the women's van, the guardsmen returned to the airport. On the following morning, the women's bodies were found and buried by nearby villagers. A local parish priest heard of the burial and notified his superior, who notified the U.S. embassy.

Many North Americans' first memory of El Salvador is the shocking footage on the nightly news of the churchwomen's bodies being dragged by ropes from their graves. Then-U.S. Ambassador Robert White, present at the exhumation, was, like many, deeply upset and vowed that "this time they won't get away with it. They just won't." On May 24, 1985, the five National Guardsmen (but not their commander) were found guilty of murder and given the maximum penalty under Salvadoran law.

That the accused even went to trial, let alone were convicted, is amazing in light of Salvadoran political and legal history and is a tribute to the ability of citizens to influence their government on an issue of importance to them. No Salvadoran military officer or enlisted man in recent memory had been tried, let alone convicted, for the murder of civilians, despite the thousands of deaths attributed to military violence over the years. Corruption and harassment of lawyers and judges prosecuting military cases are commonplace. The Salvadoran legal code makes a conviction for any crime very difficult to obtain, and lack of investigative and legal skills is an enormous impediment, even without the political problems. Michael Posner, the legal representative of the churchwomen's families and director of the Lawyers Committee for International Human Rights, believes that the families would never have seen justice done without the enormous attention paid to this case by a diverse and vocal public. State Department and congressional staffers close to the case agree that it was the great public pressure on them that moved the case to resolution. Although individuals in the bureaucracy were committed to prosecution of the guilty, it took attention by the media and a concentrated public focus to force the institutions to spend the countless hours needed to pressure and assist the Salvadorans in the myriad details of investigation and trial preparation.

How did the public become concerned about this case, and what did they do to express this concern?

The religious community and human-rights groups spontaneously became actively involved in the case. Religious leaders, missionaries, and lay workers from all religions felt personally threatened when innocent colleagues were murdered for their humanitarian work. The Maryknoll Order headquarters in Ossining, New York, received countless phone calls, letters, and requests for speakers from religious groups across the country. The religious press also reported on the case and kept its readership informed of the latest developments and the need for continued support. From the letters that were received by Congress and the State Department, it is apparent that many citizens learned about the churchwomen's case from the pulpit and took the initiative to write about their concern.

Congress, as a representative body, had little choice but to react to the inquiries that came into members' offices. But it wasn't only letters that sparked their interest in the case. Senators Claiborne Pell (Democrat-Rhode Island) and Charles Percy (Republican-Illinois), respectively Minority and, then, Majority leaders of the Senate Foreign Relations Committee, arrived in their offices one day to find Maryknoll sisters holding a sit-in. Other members of Congress, with a special interest in human rights or a strong Catholic background, became involved. Cleveland-area representative Mary Rose Oakar, a former classmate of one of the women, was a key congressional actor in the case from beginning to end. Citizens, some unconnected to any church and not particularly political, wrote or stopped by congressmen's offices to ask for speedy justice and an end to all U.S. aid until a conviction was obtained.

In September 1981, Congress approved language that made progress in the churchwomen's case a crucial element of the "certification law." This law required President Reagan to evaluate and certify every 180 days that the Salvadoran government and armed forces were making progress toward political and economic reform and respect for human rights. The certification law and the accompanying congressional hearings provided the families of the churchwomen a natural forum in which to present their case to the Congress, the press, and the public. Entire hearings focused on the case to the exclusion of other non-human-rights issues. If progress had been found lacking, the president could have been forced to cut off military and economic assistance. The certification law served as a congressional guideline for U.S. policy in El Salvador until it was defeated in Congress in April 1984.

The case seemed irreversibly stalled on several occasions. Initially, the Salvadoran military blocked action because of fear of the consequences of a complete investigation and trial. A U.S. embassy officer, at great risk, made a personal commitment to break the case and identify the murderers. The embassy presented his evidence to the Salvadoran government and demanded the arrest of the five National Guardsmen identified by the embassy officer in April 1981. Preparation for the trial stalled for several months in 1982-1983, when the Salvadoran judiciary and government failed to conduct a proper investigation and to document the evidence.

The churchwomen's families and their legal representatives became convinced that they had to take matters into their own hands. Michael Posner says that by early 1982 the families realized that the information the U.S. government had or gave was limited, so they decided to conduct their own investigation. Posner and William Ford, brother of Ita Ford, went to El Salvador for the first time in January 1982. Eight subsequent trips were made on behalf of the families, each time resulting in more effective and aggressive pressure on the State Department and the Salvadoran government. According to Posner, there were many times when the families identified a lead, or evidence for the trial, and requested the U.S. embassy to follow up formally with the Salvadoran government. In this way, the families developed close working relationships with the State Department, the U.S. embassy in El Salvador, and with sympathetic Salvadorans who also wanted to see justice done.

This initiative helped generate congressional pressure for an independent investigation to provide Congress and the families with information about U.S. and Salvadoran efforts to achieve justice in the case. In May 1983, the State Department asked a former federal judge to conduct an independent review of the evidence in the case. This so-called Tyler Report, while praising the State Department and criticizing the Salvadorans' handling of the case, made crucial recommendations that, when carried out, tightened the evidence against the guardsmen.

Another significant signal of the public's and Congress' acute interest in the case was passage of an amendment offered by Republican senator Arlen Specter, a former district attorney of Philadelphia, in November 1983. After being approached by the churchwomen's families and legal representatives, Senator Specter pushed for passage of this amendment, which withheld 30 percent of authorized 1983 military assistance to El Salvador until a conviction in the churchwomen's case was obtained. The Spector amendment expressed Congress' feelings about the importance of seeing justice done and of establishing a legal and political precedent for prosecuting human-rights violators. Senator Spector's legal training and prosecutor's instincts led him to track events closely and to press the Salvadorans personally on several occasions.

The press also played a crucial role in investigating new leads and reporting new developments in the case. The families encouraged this interest by giving press conferences and cultivating contacts. The Donovan family made television talk-show appearances and traveled across the country speaking about the case and U.S.-Salvadoran relations. Three movies were made about the life of Jean Donovan, helping to personalize the case for thousands of Americans.

Lesson: After the murders, the families, who all had faith in their government, were shocked and dismayed when the case did not proceed smoothly. None of the family members was particularly political until the radicalizing experience of pushing the U.S. government far beyond where it would naturally go. Now William Ford is called upon weekly to discuss the case, to serve on boards, and to support others in the human-rights struggle. The family and their close supporters, sometimes spontaneously and sometimes in a well-organized manner, employed various strategies—insider, outsider, and radical outsider—to influence policy. By using these various strategies they reached segments of all three publics: opinion makers, the attentive, and, eventually, the mass public.

The families talked to local, state, and national media and to political leaders on all levels of government. They tried to personalize the issue for other citizens. Some churchwomen adopted the radical strategy of holding sit-ins in congressional offices, and the more established strategy of writing letters to Washington officials. They used insiders in Congress to broaden the constituency calling for justice. But it took interest from mainstream Americans, especially those supportive of the administration, to move the executive branch. Indeed, an issue gets particular attention when any administration's special constituency responds to it. Ultimately, it was the moral revulsion over the violation of religious workers, and the hard work of the families and their representatives, that brought the five National Guardsmen to trial and allowed their conviction. (In contrast, the cases of nine of the eleven other Americans killed in El Salvador have not gone very far in the Congress, with the human-rights community, the State Department, or in El Salvador. And no Salvadoran military officer or enlisted man has yet to be convicted for the thousands of violations of the human rights of Salvadoran citizens by the armed forces since 1979.)

A FINAL NOTE ON CONSENSUS

As we have said several times in this book, U.S. foreign policy is conducted best when there is a relative consensus among concerned citizens about the direction in which their country should be going. Such a consensus appears to have developed during 1985 in Washington about U.S. policy toward El Salvador and, to a lesser extent, toward Nicaragua. But only about one-fourth of the generalpublic know what that policy is. In urging you to inform yourself better about Central America and to try to make your voice heard in Washington, we would like to add one other consideration: that you think not only about what you believe the United States should be doing in Central America but also about that set of policies that are acceptable to your neighbors, colleagues, parents, and children.

There are no easy choices in Central America; all options involve some risks for U.S. interests and dangers for the people of the region. We hope that as you become more actively involved in the issue of Central America you will go through the mental exercise performed in writing this book: trying to see the world through the eyes of someone with a very different point of view. Such an exercise does not produce instant agreement and it should not produce inaction. But it should cause at least a momentary humility about the ability of any single human being to have the right answer to every problem. Use your understanding of other people's point of view to argue more effectively, to persuade if you can, and, ultimately, to compromise if you must.

Whatever the merits of any approach to the problems of Central America, no policy will be successful if it is not sustainable over a long period. In a democracy this means that many people, from very different regions, walks of life, and political persuasions must come together in rough agreement. We hope we have persuaded you that the problems of Central America merit your attention. As a final editorial comment, let us express the hope that you will find the opinions of your fellow citizens worthy of your attention as well.

Index

INDEX